Learning HSK words with puzzles

Level: HSK 1

by

Elle Lin

ISBN: 978-615-01-6235-5 (paperback)

TABLE OF CONTENTS

Introduction

With the help of this puzzle workbook, you can practice the vocabulary necessary for the HSK 1 exam.

The book is split into two parts.

The vocabulary needed to pass the *HSK Level 1* of the so-called *"New HSK 2.0"* is found in part one, that is, in Units 1 through 6, and the first revision. Despite being declared obsolete in 2021, this "New HSK 2.0" was still in use when this book was written.

However, to practice all the words needed for the *HSK Level 1* of the *"New HSK 3.0"* announced in March 2021, you have to work your way through the entire book, that is, through the first and second parts as well.

Including the four revisions, the book is broken up into 25 units. In total, there are 125 exercises in it. In our opinion, using puzzles to practice vocabulary makes the process much easier. As a result, the book contains exercises like matching games, word searches (character searches), crossword puzzles, word fill-ins, etc.

The *21 units containing new words* are structured as follows:

- A *vocabulary list* with new characters, their Pinyin, and their English meanings appears on the first page of every unit. We suggest that you familiarize yourself with them and write down the characters a few times. In this manner, you will start to memorize them right away.
- Every time, the *first puzzle* is a matching game that tests your recall of the words from the previous page.
- In the *second puzzle*, you have to find hidden Chinese characters in a word search puzzle so that you can use some of them to finish off a sentence.

- The *third one* is always a crossword puzzle, where you test yourself on how well you remember the English meaning of the Chinese words.
- The *fourth one* is a fill-in exercise, where you have to complete a crossword by entering the Pinyin of the given Chinese words. However, this time we show you hints of the tones in some of the squares rather than giving you clear cues as to where the words should go.
- The *fifth puzzle* is either a Letter Cloud, where you must use given letters to form Pinyin words, or a quiz, where you have to find out which one of the provided words is correct.

In case of the ***revisions***:
- The *first exercise* requires you to build Chinese characters out of the provided components.
- The *second exercise* requires you to match pictures with their corresponding Chinese words.
- The *third exercise* is a crossword.
- The *fourth exercise* is another fill-in exercise with provided hints on the proper tones of the Pinyin words that should be entered into the squares.
- The *fifth exercise* in the review units requires you to sort a set of words according to their meaning.

The book was created to be a HSK word practice workbook; grammar exercises are not included. Therefore, in order to develop the necessary grammar skills, you cannot avoid going through a textbook as well.

I think it's possible for learning to be entertaining, and I hope you will enjoy and benefit from the exercises in this book. So, let's start your learning journey!

Have fun!

Elle Lin

Part One

UNIT 1
VOCABULARY

1.	一	yī	one
2.	二	èr	two
3.	十	shí	ten
4.	七	qī	seven
5.	人	rén	people
6.	八	bā	eight
7.	九	jiǔ	nine
8.	儿子	érzi	son
9.	几	jǐ	several, a few
10.	了	le	past tense marker
11.	三	sān	three
12.	工作	gōngzuò	work
13.	下	xià	below; under; next
14.	下午	xiàwǔ	afternoon
15.	下雨	xià yǔ	to rain
16.	大	dà	large, big
17.	上	shàng	upper, above
18.	上午	shàngwǔ	morning
19.	个	gè	measure word
20.	女儿	nǚ'ér	daughter
21.	飞机	fēijī	plane
22.	开	kāi	to open
23.	不	bù	no, not
24.	不客气	bú kèqi	you're welcome
25.	少	shǎo	less, few

Match the Hanzi with the corresponding Pinyin and English translation.

#	Hanzi		Pinyin		English
1.	一	☐	bā	☐	afternoon
2.	二	☐	bù	☐	below; under; next
3.	十	☐	bú kèqi	☐	daughter
4.	七	☐	dà	☐	eight
5.	人	☐	èr	☐	large, big
6.	八	☐	érzi	☐	less, few
7.	九	☐	fēijī	☐	measure word
8.	儿子	☐	gè	☐	morning
9.	几	☐	gōngzuò	☐	nine
10.	了	☐	jǐ	☐	no, not
11.	三	☐	jiǔ	☐	one
12.	工作	☐	kāi	☐	past tense marker
13.	下	☐	le	☐	people
14.	下午	☐	nǚ'ér	☐	plane
15.	下雨	☐	qī	☐	seven
16.	大	☐	rén	☐	several, a few
17.	上	☐	sān	☐	son
18.	上午	☐	shàng	☐	ten
19.	个	☐	shàngwǔ	☐	three
20.	女儿	☐	shǎo	☐	to open
21.	飞机	☐	shí	☐	to rain
22.	开	☐	xià	☐	two
23.	不	☐	xiàwǔ	☐	upper, above
24.	不客气	☐	xià yǔ	☐	work
25.	少	☐	yī	☐	You're welcome

Once ready, check your solution with the help of the previous page.

Find the Chinese characters belonging to the following Pinyin words. In the grid, words with multiple characters can appear either vertically from top to bottom, or horizontally from left to right.

bā	érzi	jiǔ	rén	shí
bù	fēijī	kāi	sān	xià
bú kèqi	gè	le	shàng	xiàwǔ
dà	gōngzuò	nǚ'ér	shàngwǔ	xià yǔ
èr	jǐ	qī	shǎo	yī

月	写	大	有	你	下	雨	怎	么	样	认	上
会	名	汉	八	零	漂	亮	三	没	不	识	桌
下	字	语	他	冷	水	果	同	学	高	九	子
午	火	几	出	租	车	下	昨	儿	兴	门	开
本	车	中	国	爸	二	再	天	子	没	口	商
了	站	叫	少	爸	电	见	衣	服	关	飞	店
医	十	喝	吃	回	影	一	前	面	系	机	去
院	书	苹	工	作	在	日	杯	子	了	女	下
个	岁	果	说	话	山	女	儿	能	明	钱	午
老	师	东	西	七	我	们	年	人	天	上	学
现	大	茶	这	很	后	面	饭	馆	住	午	习
在	星	期	北	京	热	猫	不	客	气	请	呢

A few Hanzi belonging to the Pinyin words above can be found twice in the grid. Take one of the pairs and insert them into the empty spaces below so that you get a meaningful sentence.

今天　□　□　下 了 很 □ 的 雨。

Put the English translation of the Chinese words into the squares. If the English translation contains more than one word, you must enter them without space into the squares.

Across

1. 飞机
5. 女儿
6. 下雨
8. 二
12. 三
13. 上
14. 上午
16. 一
17. 十
21. 不客气
22. 九
23. 人

Down

2. 八
3. 大
4. 儿子
7. 下午
9. 工作
10. 下
11. 开
15. 几
18. 七
19. 少
20. 不

Complete the crossword by entering the Pinyin of the supplied Chinese words. However, this time, instead of providing you with clear indications as to where the words should go, we show you hints of the tones in some of the squares.

二 _______________   下午 _______________

人 _______________   下雨 _______________

八 _______________   上 _______________

九 _______________   上午 _______________

儿子 _______________   个 _______________

几 _______________   女儿 _______________

三 _______________   开 _______________

工作 _______________   少 _______________

Create Pinyin words from the letters found in the letter cloud and
write them next to their English translation. You can use each letter only once.

seven   _________________________

not   _________________________

big   _________________________

ten   _________________________

airplane   _________________________

past tense   _________________________

you're welcome   _________________________

one   _________________________

If you did a good job, by now there should be only two unused letters left
in the cloud. Make a Pinyin word out of them and write down its English translation.

UNIT 2
VOCABULARY

1.	小	xiǎo	small
2.	小姐	xiǎojiě	Miss, young lady
3.	天气	tiānqì	weather
4.	五	wǔ	five
5.	太	tài	too, excessively
6.	日	rì	date, sun
7.	中午	zhōngwǔ	noon
8.	中国	Zhōngguó	China
9.	水	shuǐ	water
10.	水果	shuǐguǒ	fruits
11.	什么	shénme	what
12.	今天	jīntiān	today
13.	分钟	fēnzhōng	minute
14.	月	yuè	month
15.	六	liù	six
16.	火车站	huǒchēzhàn	train station
17.	认识	rènshi	to know, to recognize
18.	书	shū	book
19.	打电话	dǎ diànhuà	to make a phonecall
20.	去	qù	to go
21.	本	běn	measure word for books
22.	北京	Běijīng	Beijing
23.	电视	diànshì	television
24.	电脑	diànnǎo	computer
25.	出租车	chūzūchē	taxi

Match the Hanzi with the corresponding Pinyin and English translation.

	Hanzi		Pinyin		English
1.	小	☐	Běijīng	☐	Beijing
2.	小姐	☐	běn	☐	book
3.	天气	☐	chūzūchē	☐	China
4.	五	☐	dǎ diànhuà	☐	computer
5.	太	☐	diànnǎo	☐	date, sun
6.	日	☐	diànshì	☐	five
7.	中午	☐	fēnzhōng	☐	fruits
8.	中国	☐	huǒchēzhàn	☐	measure word for books
9.	水	☐	jīntiān	☐	minute
10.	水果	☐	liù	☐	Miss, young lady
11.	什么	☐	qù	☐	month
12.	今天	☐	rènshi	☐	noon
13.	分钟	☐	rì	☐	six
14.	月	☐	shénme	☐	small
15.	六	☐	shū	☐	taxi
16.	火车站	☐	shuǐ	☐	television
17.	认识	☐	shuǐguǒ	☐	to go
18.	书	☐	tài	☐	to know, to recognize
19.	打电话	☐	tiānqì	☐	to make a phonecall
20.	去	☐	wǔ	☐	today
21.	本	☐	xiǎo	☐	too, excessively
22.	北京	☐	xiǎojiě	☐	train station
23.	电视	☐	yuè	☐	water
24.	电脑	☐	Zhōngguó	☐	weather
25.	出租车	☐	zhōngwǔ	☐	what

Once ready, check your solution with the help of the previous page.

UNIT 2
Word search

Find the Chinese characters belonging to the following Pinyin words. In the grid, words with multiple characters can appear either vertically from top to bottom, or horizontally from left to right.

Běijīng	diànshì	qù	shuǐ	xiǎo
běn	fēnzhōng	rènshi	shuǐguǒ	xiǎojiě
chūzūchē	huǒchēzhàn	rì	tài	yuè
dǎ diànhuà	jīntiān	shénme	tiānqì	Zhōngguó
diànnǎo	liù	shū	wǔ	zhōngwǔ

本	个	写	同	学	对	岁	米	饭	五	衣	下
年	七	小	姐	叫	不	北	京	三	你	服	书
上	几	在	儿	有	起	开	电	女	儿	呢	二
去	医	电	子	中	国	一	影	火	车	站	汉
再	院	脑	没	关	系	水	回	名	字	冷	语
见	小	听	中	午	今	下	午	电	后	分	钟
飞	大	不	客	气	天	他	多	视	面	今	饭
机	出	租	车	时	候	太	少	工	上	天	馆
打	了	老	师	火	四	九	月	作	午	认	识
电	东	中	先	车	什	么	会	水	下	雨	人
话	西	午	生	站	医	生	十	果	我	天	少
妈	妈	些	日	里	吗	六	八	这	们	气	不

A few Hanzi belonging to the Pinyin words above can be found twice in the grid. Take one of the pairs and insert them into the empty spaces below so that you get a meaningful sentence.

我 ☐☐☐☐ 在 ☐☐☐ 前面等你。

Put the English translation of the Chinese words into the squares. If the English translation contains more than one word, you must enter them without space into the squares.

Across

2 认识
4 小
6 天气
10 水果
11 电视
12 电脑
13 太
15 六
16 小姐
19 月
21 打电话
22 五

Down

1 水
3 什么
4 日
5 北京
7 中午
8 分钟
9 中国
11 火车站
14 书
17 去
18 今天
20 出租车

UNIT 2
Fill-in

Complete the crossword by entering the Pinyin of the supplied Chinese words.
However, this time, instead of providing you with clear indications as to where
the words should go, we show you hints of the tones in some of the squares.

五 ________

太 ________

日 ________

月 ________

六 ________

书 ________

去 ________

本 ________

小姐 ___________   什么 ___________   打电话 ___________

天气 ___________   今天 ___________   北京 ___________

中午 ___________   分钟 ___________   电视 ___________

中国 ___________   火车站 ___________   电脑 ___________

水果 ___________   认识 ___________   出租车 ___________

Create Pinyin words from the letters found in the letter cloud and
write them next to their English translation. You can use each letter only once.

to go   ________________

book   ________________

month   ________________

six   ________________

water   ________________

small   ________________

five   ________________

date, sun   ________________

If you did a good job, by now there should be only three unused letters in the cloud.
Make a Pinyin word out of them and write down its English translation!

1.	东西	dōngxi	thing
2.	电影	diànyǐng	film
3.	叫	jiào	to call; to be called
4.	四	sì	four
5.	他	tā	he
6.	汉语	Hànyǔ	Chinese language
7.	写	xiě	to write
8.	对不起	duìbuqǐ	I'm sorry.
9.	老师	lǎoshī	teacher
10.	再见	zàijiàn	bye
11.	在	zài	to be at/in; to exist
12.	有	yǒu	to have
13.	同学	tóngxué	classmate
14.	吃	chī	to eat
15.	吗	ma	auxiliary word for questions
16.	岁	suì	year, age
17.	回	huí	to go back; to return
18.	年	nián	year
19.	先生	xiānsheng	Sir, Mr.
20.	后面	hòumian	behind
21.	会	huì	can; to be able to
22.	名字	míngzi	name
23.	多	duō	many; much; more
24.	多少	duōshao	how much, how many
25.	衣服	yīfu	clothes

Match the Hanzi with the corresponding Pinyin and English translation.

	Hanzi		Pinyin		English
1.	东西	☐	chī	☐	auxiliary word for questions
2.	电影	☐	diànyǐng	☐	behind
3.	叫	☐	dōngxi	☐	bye
4.	四	☐	duìbuqǐ	☐	can; to be able to
5.	他	☐	duō	☐	Chinese language
6.	汉语	☐	duōshao	☐	classmate
7.	写	☐	Hànyǔ	☐	clothes
8.	对不起	☐	hòumian	☐	film
9.	老师	☐	huí	☐	four
10.	再见	☐	huì	☐	he
11.	在	☐	jiào	☐	how much, how many
12.	有	☐	lǎoshī	☐	I'm sorry.
13.	同学	☐	ma	☐	many; much; more
14.	吃	☐	míngzi	☐	name
15.	吗	☐	nián	☐	Sir, Mr.
16.	岁	☐	sì	☐	teacher
17.	回	☐	suì	☐	thing
18.	年	☐	tā	☐	to be at/in; to exist
19.	先生	☐	tóngxué	☐	to call; to be called
20.	后面	☐	xiānsheng	☐	to eat
21.	会	☐	xiě	☐	to go back; to return
22.	名字	☐	yīfu	☐	to have
23.	多	☐	yǒu	☐	to write
24.	多少	☐	zài	☐	year
25.	衣服	☐	zàijiàn	☐	year, age

Once ready, check your solution with the help of the previous page.

Find the Chinese characters belonging to the following Pinyin words. In the grid, words with multiple characters can appear either vertically from top to bottom, or horizontally from left to right.

chī	duōshao	jiào	sì	xiě
diànyǐng	Hànyǔ	lǎoshī	suì	yīfu
dōngxi	hòumian	ma	tā	yǒu
duìbuqǐ	huí	míngzi	tóngxué	zài
duō	huì	nián	xiānsheng	zàijiàn

电	脑	你	杯	看	五	先	生	昨	天	他	看
多	本	回	子	见	听	中	里	打	电	话	六
今	星	期	对	不	起	国	汉	语	些	东	学
天	吃	我	们	她	能	什	北	京	书	西	校
分	钟	医	生	名	字	么	岁	钱	中	水	果
会	学	电	饭	馆	学	习	我	在	午	叫	月
住	生	影	水	写	呢	他	电	视	有	好	妈
衣	时	候	来	高	米	饭	那	四	小	块	妈
服	这	再	见	兴	明	天	天	气	姐	同	学
坐	吗	没	关	系	叫	朋	老	师	火	车	站
名	说	话	后	认	小	友	医	院	出	租	车
字	热	少	面	识	爱	多	少	太	家	年	是

A few Hanzi belonging to the Pinyin words above can be found twice in the grid. Take one of the pairs and insert them into the empty spaces below so that you get a meaningful sentence.

UNIT 3
Crossword

Put the English translation of the Chinese words into the squares. If the English translation contains more than one word, you must enter them without space into the squares.

Across

2 多少   15 四
5 东西   16 回
8 同学   17 多
9 岁   19 再见
10 先生   20 老师
13 有

Down

1 电影   10 对不起
3 写   11 汉语
4 他   12 后面
6 吃   14 衣服
7 年   18 名字
8 叫   21 会

UNIT 3
Fill-in

Complete the crossword by entering the Pinyin of the supplied Chinese words.
This time, instead of providing you with clear indications as to where
the words should go, we show you hints of the tones in some of the squares.

东西 _______

电影 _______

叫 _______

四 _______

他 _______

汉语 _______

写 _______

对不起 _______

老师 _______

再见 _______

在 _______

有 _______

同学 _______

吃 _______

吗 _______

岁 _______

回 _______

年 _______

先生 _______

后面 _______

会 _______

名字 _______

多 _______

多少 _______

衣服 _______

UNIT 3
Letter Cloud

Create Pinyin words from the letters found in the letter cloud and
write them next to their English translation. You can use each letter only once.

M Y F G I H Ǒ
O H Y J Í U U C
I Ō I U N N
A I N I X I Á Ě
U N Z D

to have   _____________________

clothes   _____________________

name   _____________________

year   _____________________

to call, to be called   _____________________

to eat   _____________________

many, much   _____________________

to write   _____________________

If you did a good job, by now there should be only three unused letters in the cloud.
Make a Pinyin word out of them and write down its English translation!

_________   _____________________

UNIT 4
VOCABULARY

1.	米饭	mǐfàn	(steamed/cooked) rice
2.	字	zì	word; Chinese character
3.	那	nà	that
4.	好	hǎo	good
5.	她	tā	she
6.	妈妈	māma	mother
7.	买	mǎi	to buy
8.	块	kuài	piece
9.	医生	yīshēng	doctor
10.	医院	yīyuàn	hospital
11.	来	lái	to come
12.	时候	shíhou	time
13.	里	lǐ	in, inside
14.	听	tīng	to hear
15.	我	wǒ	I
16.	我们	wǒmen	we
17.	你	nǐ	you
18.	饭馆	fànguǎn	restaurant
19.	冷	lěng	cold
20.	没	méi	no
21.	没关系	méi guānxi	No problem.
22.	苹果	píngguǒ	apple
23.	杯子	bēizi	cup
24.	明天	míngtiān	tomorrow
25.	呢	ne	aux. word for asking back

Match the Hanzi with the corresponding Pinyin and English translation.

	Hanzi		Pinyin		English
1.	米饭	☐	bēizi	☐	(steamed/cooked) rice
2.	字	☐	fànguǎn	☐	apple
3.	那	☐	hǎo	☐	aux. word for asking back
4.	好	☐	kuài	☐	cold
5.	她	☐	lái	☐	cup
6.	妈妈	☐	lěng	☐	doctor
7.	买	☐	lǐ	☐	good
8.	块	☐	māma	☐	hospital
9.	医生	☐	mǎi	☐	I
10.	医院	☐	méi	☐	in, inside
11.	来	☐	méi guānxi	☐	mother
12.	时候	☐	mǐfàn	☐	no
13.	里	☐	míngtiān	☐	No problem.
14.	听	☐	nà	☐	piece
15.	我	☐	ne	☐	restaurant
16.	我们	☐	nǐ	☐	she
17.	你	☐	píngguǒ	☐	that
18.	饭馆	☐	shíhou	☐	time
19.	冷	☐	tā	☐	to buy
20.	没	☐	tīng	☐	to come
21.	没关系	☐	wǒ	☐	to hear
22.	苹果	☐	wǒmen	☐	tomorrow
23.	杯子	☐	yīshēng	☐	we
24.	明天	☐	yīyuàn	☐	word; Chinese character
25.	呢	☐	zì	☐	you

Once ready, check your solution with the help of the previous page.

Find the Chinese characters belonging to the following Pinyin words. In the grid, words with multiple characters can appear either vertically from top to bottom, or horizontally from left to right.

bēizi	lěng	méi guānxi	nǐ	wǒ
fànguǎn	lǐ	mǐfàn	píngguǒ	wǒmen
hǎo	māma	míngtiān	shíhou	yīshēng
kuài	mǎi	nà	tā	yīyuàn
lái	méi	ne	tīng	zì

妈	妈	想	字	看	见	漂	分	饭	前	喝	你
小	学	生	下	车	买	亮	钟	馆	面	医	院
干	我	喜	欢	里	去	中	杯	茶	叫	来	很
读	们	猫	上	电	水	午	子	狗	苹	汉	是
妈	谢	好	边	脑	医	院	多	少	果	语	哪
妈	谢	一	样	东	西	朋	商	店	小	学	习
也	月	时	候	看	下	友	冷	怎	时	医	生
没	谁	电	星	块	次	那	大	么	一	会	儿
门	老	视	期	椅	上	网	学	样	呢	学	生
口	师	明	工	子	听	山	明	天	睡	觉	她
小	姐	天	人	飞	零	车	门	米	饭	今	能
我	和	做	菜	没	关	系	票	认	识	天	书

A few Hanzi belonging to the Pinyin words above can be found twice in the grid. Take one of the pairs and insert them into the empty spaces below so that you get a meaningful sentence.

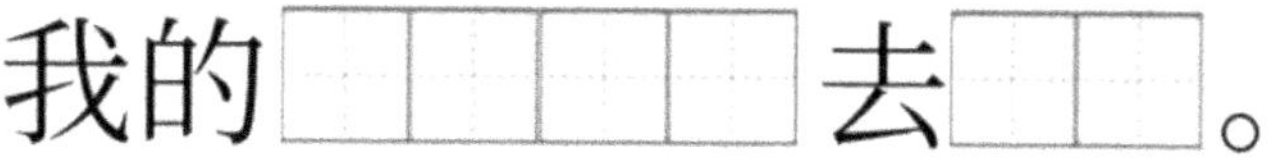

Put the English translation of the Chinese words into the squares. If the English translation contains more than one word, you must enter them without space into the squares.

Across

1 饭馆
4 听
5 块
6 明天
7 里
9 医生
11 字
12 来
15 买
16 医院
19 冷
20 妈妈
21 我们

Down

2 米饭
3 那
8 没关系
10 她
12 杯子
13 好
14 苹果
17 时候
18 你

Complete the crossword by entering the Pinyin of the supplied Chinese words.
This time, instead of providing you with clear indications as to where
the words should go, we show you hints of the tones in some of the squares.

字 _______
那 _______
好 _______
她 _______
买 _______
块 _______
来 _______
里 _______
听 _______
我 _______
你 _______
冷 _______

没 _______
呢 _______
米饭 _______
妈妈 _______
医生 _______
时候 _______

我们 _______
饭馆 _______
没关系 _______
苹果 _______
明天 _______
杯子 _______

UNIT 4
Letter Cloud

Create Pinyin words from the letters found in the letter cloud and
write them next to their English translation. You can use each letter only once.

to come _________________

to buy _________________

to hear _________________

I _________________

doctor _________________

cold _________________

you _________________

apple _________________

If you did a good job, by now there should be only three unused letters in the cloud.
Make a Pinyin word out of them and write down its English translation!

_________________ _________________

#	汉字	拼音	英文
1.	住	zhù	to live, to dwell
2.	坐	zuò	to sit
3.	这	zhè	this
4.	现在	xiànzài	now
5.	些	xiē	a few
6.	和	hé	and
7.	的	de	of
8.	爸爸	bàba	dad
9.	朋友	péngyou	friend
10.	狗	gǒu	dog
11.	学习	xuéxí	to study
12.	学生	xué•shēng	student
13.	学校	xuéxiào	school
14.	茶	chá	tea
15.	点	diǎn	spot
16.	是	shì	to be; yes
17.	星期	xīngqī	week
18.	昨天	zuótiān	yesterday
19.	哪	nǎ	which
20.	看	kàn	to see
21.	很	hěn	very
22.	都	dōu	all
23.	爱	ài	to love
24.	高兴	gāoxìng	happy
25.	读	dú	to read

Match the Hanzi with the corresponding Pinyin and English translation.

#	Hanzi		Pinyin		English
1.	住	☐	ài	☐	a few
2.	坐	☐	bàba	☐	all
3.	这	☐	chá	☐	and
4.	现在	☐	de	☐	dad
5.	些	☐	diǎn	☐	dog
6.	和	☐	dōu	☐	friend
7.	的	☐	dú	☐	happy
8.	爸爸	☐	gāoxìng	☐	now
9.	朋友	☐	gǒu	☐	of
10.	狗	☐	hé	☐	school
11.	学习	☐	hěn	☐	spot
12.	学生	☐	kàn	☐	student
13.	学校	☐	nǎ	☐	tea
14.	茶	☐	péngyou	☐	this
15.	点	☐	shì	☐	to be; yes
16.	是	☐	xiànzài	☐	to live, to dwell
17.	星期	☐	xiē	☐	to love
18.	昨天	☐	xīngqī	☐	to read
19.	哪	☐	xué • shēng	☐	to see
20.	看	☐	xuéxí	☐	to sit
21.	很	☐	xuéxiào	☐	to study
22.	都	☐	zhè	☐	very
23.	爱	☐	zhù	☐	week
24.	高兴	☐	zuò	☐	which
25.	读	☐	zuótiān	☐	yesterday

Once ready, check your solution with the help of the previous page.

Find the Chinese characters belonging to the following Pinyin words. In the grid, words with multiple characters can appear either vertically from top to bottom, or horizontally from left to right.

ài	dōu	hěn	xiànzài	xuéxiào
bàba	dú	kàn	xiē	zhè
chá	gāoxìng	nǎ	xīngqī	zhù
de	gǒu	péngyou	xuéshēng	zuò
diǎn	hé	shì	xuéxí	zuótiān

名	字	昨	回	同	高	中	叫	汉	些	会	吗
这	吃	天	去	学	兴	国	茶	语	飞	她	点
先	中	午	开	的	电	脑	今	爸	机	小	姐
生	学	生	不	对	不	起	天	爸	五	很	七
朋	下	雨	狗	不	星	期	四	打	个	衣	服
友	爱	上	午	客	再	见	很	电	朋	十	火
认	小	太	是	气	大	住	水	话	友	六	车
识	和	水	果	高	兴	九	的	本	天	气	站
狗	分	钟	学	女	儿	现	写	哪	北	看	电
儿	少	上	习	什	块	在	月	后	京	东	视
子	学	那	妈	么	老	米	读	面	坐	西	好
日	校	来	年	都	师	饭	听	有	书	现	在

A few Hanzi belonging to the Pinyin words above can be found twice in the grid. Take one of the pairs and insert them into the empty spaces below so that you get a meaningful sentence.

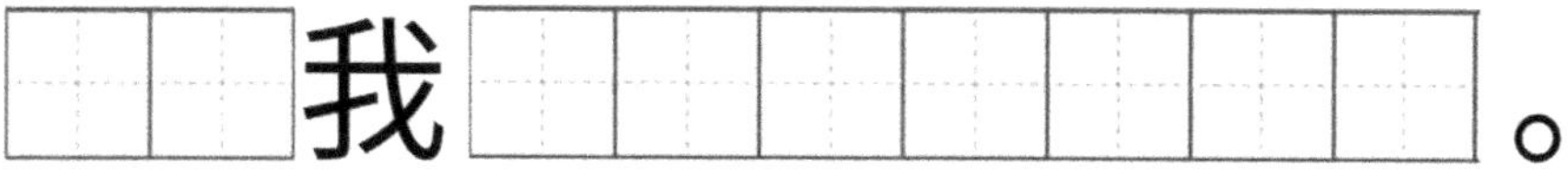

Put the English translation of the Chinese words into the squares. If the English translation contains more than one word, you must enter them without space into the squares.

Across

2 看
4 都
8 爱
10 学习
11 些
12 星期
13 这
14 学生
15 现在
17 读
19 高兴
20 爸爸
21 学校

Down

1 茶
2 坐
3 很
5 住
6 狗
7 昨天
9 点
11 朋友
16 哪
18 和
22 的

UNIT 5
Fill-in

Use Pinyin to put the translations of the English words into the grids. As you can see, you have to figure out where the words should go, but the tonal cues can help you in your efforts.

a few, all, and, dad, dog, friend, happy, now, of, school, spot, student, tea,
to be, to dwell, to love, to read, to see, to sit, to study, very, week, which, yesterday

Once ready, insert the words marked with asterisks into the empty spaces below so that you get a meaningful sentence.

我＿＿＿＿＿在＿＿旁边。

Create words from the letters found in the letter cloud and
write them next to their English translation. You can use each letter only once.

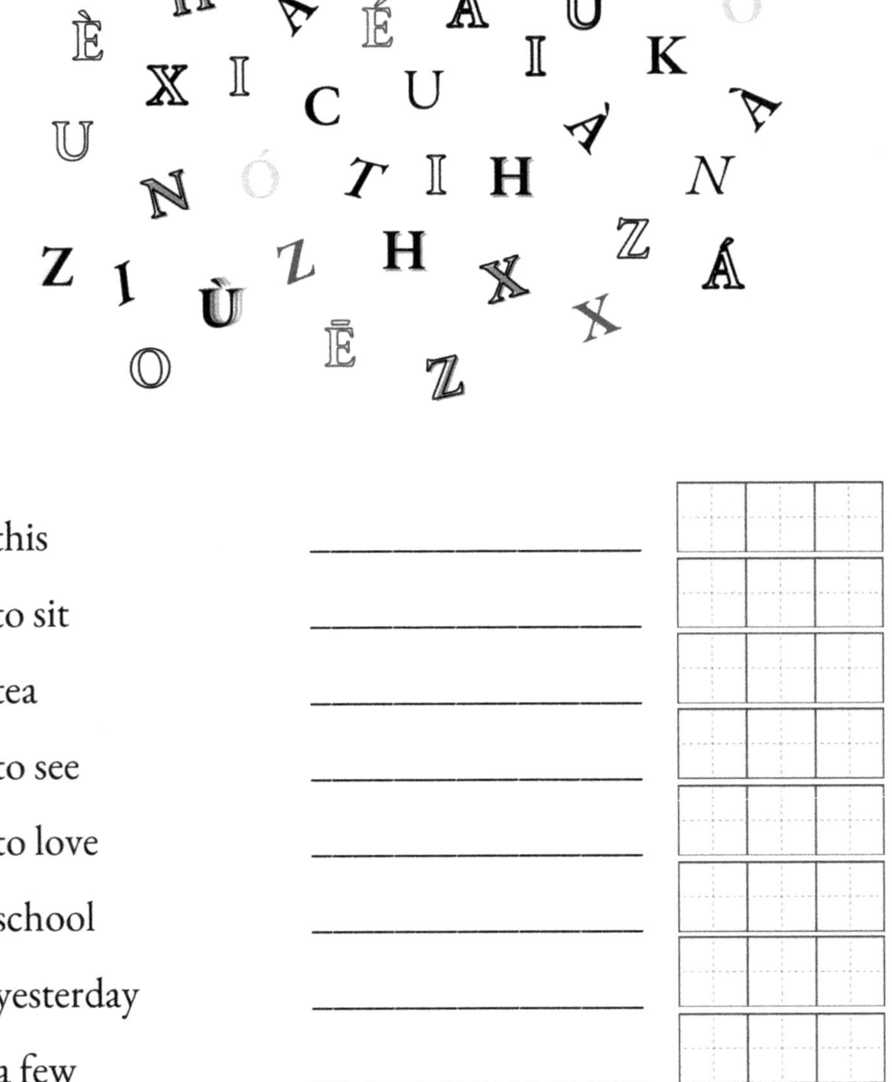

this   ___________________

to sit   ___________________

tea   ___________________

to see   ___________________

to love   ___________________

school   ___________________

yesterday   ___________________

a few   ___________________

If you did a good job, by now there should be only three unused letters in the cloud.
Make a Pinyin word out of them and write down its English translation.

___________   ___________________________

1.	看见	kàn//jiàn	to see, to catch sight of
2.	怎么	zěnme	how
3.	怎么样	zěnmeyàng	how about
4.	前面	qiánmian	in front
5.	说话	shuō//huà	to talk
6.	热	rè	heat; hot
7.	桌子	zhuōzi	table
8.	钱	qián	money
9.	家	jiā	home, family
10.	请	qǐng	please
11.	谁	shéi, shuí	who
12.	能	néng	can
13.	菜	cài	dish, vegetable
14.	做	zuò	to do, to make
15.	猫	māo	cat
16.	商店	shāngdiàn	shop
17.	喜欢	xǐhuan	to like
18.	椅子	yǐzi	chair
19.	喝	hē	to drink
20.	喂	wèi	hello, hey
21.	谢谢	xièxie	thank you
22.	想	xiǎng	to think; to want
23.	零｜〇	líng	zero
24.	睡觉	shuì//jiào	to sleep
25.	漂亮	piàoliang	pretty, beautiful

Match the Hanzi with the corresponding Pinyin and English translation.

#	Hanzi		Pinyin		English
1.	看见	☐	cài	☐	can
2.	怎么	☐	hē	☐	cat
3.	怎么样	☐	jiā	☐	chair
4.	前面	☐	kàn//jiàn	☐	dish, vegetable
5.	说话	☐	líng	☐	heat; hot
6.	热	☐	māo	☐	hello, hey
7.	桌子	☐	néng	☐	home, family
8.	钱	☐	piàoliang	☐	how
9.	家	☐	qián	☐	how about
10.	请	☐	qiánmian	☐	in front
11.	谁	☐	qǐng	☐	money
12.	能	☐	rè	☐	please
13.	菜	☐	shāngdiàn	☐	pretty, beautiful
14.	做	☐	shéi, shuí	☐	shop
15.	猫	☐	shuì//jiào	☐	table
16.	商店	☐	shuō//huà	☐	thank you
17.	喜欢	☐	wèi	☐	to do, to make
18.	椅子	☐	xiǎng	☐	to drink
19.	喝	☐	xièxie	☐	to like
20.	喂	☐	xǐhuan	☐	to see, to catch sight of
21.	谢谢	☐	yǐzi	☐	to sleep
22.	想	☐	zěnme	☐	to talk
23.	零丨○	☐	zěnmeyàng	☐	to think; to want
24.	睡觉	☐	zhuōzi	☐	who
25.	漂亮	☐	zuò	☐	zero

Once ready, check your solution with the help of the previous page.

Find the Chinese characters belonging to the following Pinyin words. In the grid, words with multiple characters can appear either vertically from top to bottom, or horizontally from left to right.

cài	māo	qǐng	shuōhuà	yǐzi
hē	néng	rè	wèi	zěnme
jiā	piàoliang	shāngdiàn	xiǎng	zěnmeyàng
kànjiàn	qián	shéi, shuí	xièxie	zhuōzi
líng	qiánmian	shuìjiào	xǐhuan	zuò

茶	坐	菜	呢	我	商	住	妈	很	谁	些	多
现	猫	和	说	话	店	做	妈	都	漂	亮	少
在	医	生	读	学	你	明	怎	么	听	谢	谢
椅	子	后	喂	生	漂	天	在	朋	友	杯	爱
昨	天	面	饭	有	亮	岁	商	她	回	子	前
苹	果	怎	馆	家	我	爸	店	多	看	学	面
零	里	么	的	吗	们	爸	块	冷	见	校	医
是	狗	样	会	喝	好	喜	欢	来	米	热	院
桌	同	学	时	星	期	高	学	四	饭	没	看
子	年	睡	候	写	想	兴	习	前	面	关	猫
再	看	觉	名	请	哪	他	衣	服	字	系	先
见	见	吃	字	那	买	这	能	点	钱	叫	生

A few Hanzi belonging to the Pinyin words above can be found twice in the grid. Take one of the pairs and insert them into the empty spaces below so that you get a meaningful sentence.

我在□□□□□□了一只□□的□。

UNIT 6
Crossword

Put the English translation of the Chinese words into the squares. If the English translation contains more than one word, you must enter them without space into the squares.

Across

1 商店
6 漂亮
7 喂
8 家
10 热
12 钱
13 说话
15 猫
18 喜欢
19 前面
21 零

Down

1 看见
2 菜
3 请
4 椅子
5 怎么样
9 谁
11 谢谢
12 做
14 想
15 能
16 睡觉
17 喝
20 桌子

UNIT 6
Fill-in

Complete the crossword by entering the Pinyin of the supplied Chinese words.
This time, instead of providing you with clear indications as to where
the words should go, we show you hints of the tones in some of the squares.

热 ______
钱 ______
家 ______
请 ______
谁 ______
能 ______
菜 ______
做 ______
猫 ______
喝 ______
喂 ______
想 ______
零 ______

看见 ______
怎么样 ______
前面 ______
说话 ______
桌子 ______
商店 ______

喜欢 ______
椅子 ______
谢谢 ______
睡觉 ______
漂亮 ______

Create Pinyin words from the letters found in the letter cloud and
write them next to their English translation. You can use each letter only once.

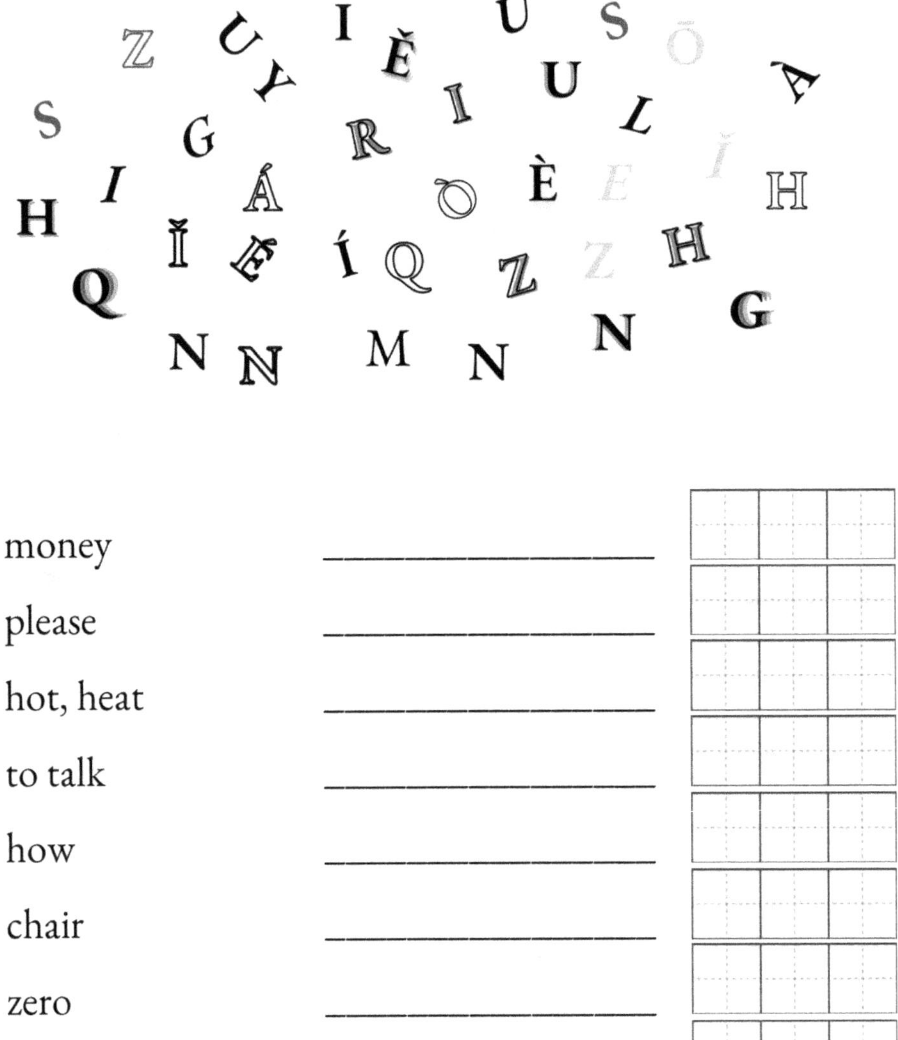

money _______________________

please _______________________

hot, heat _______________________

to talk _______________________

how _______________________

chair _______________________

zero _______________________

who _______________________

If you did a good job, by now there should be only three unused letters in the cloud.
Make a Pinyin word out of them and write down its English translation!

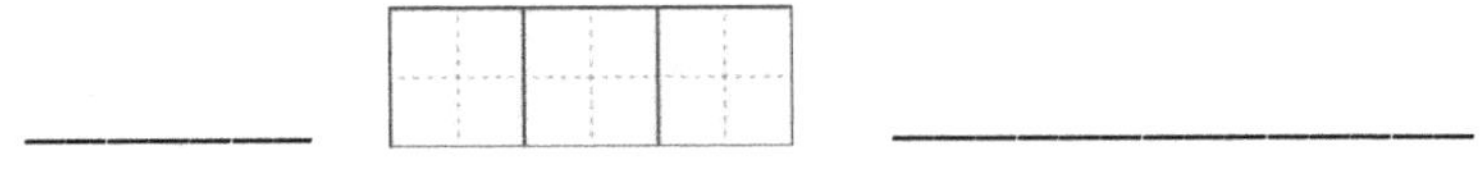

_______   _______________

REVISION
Characters

Create Chinese characters from the components.

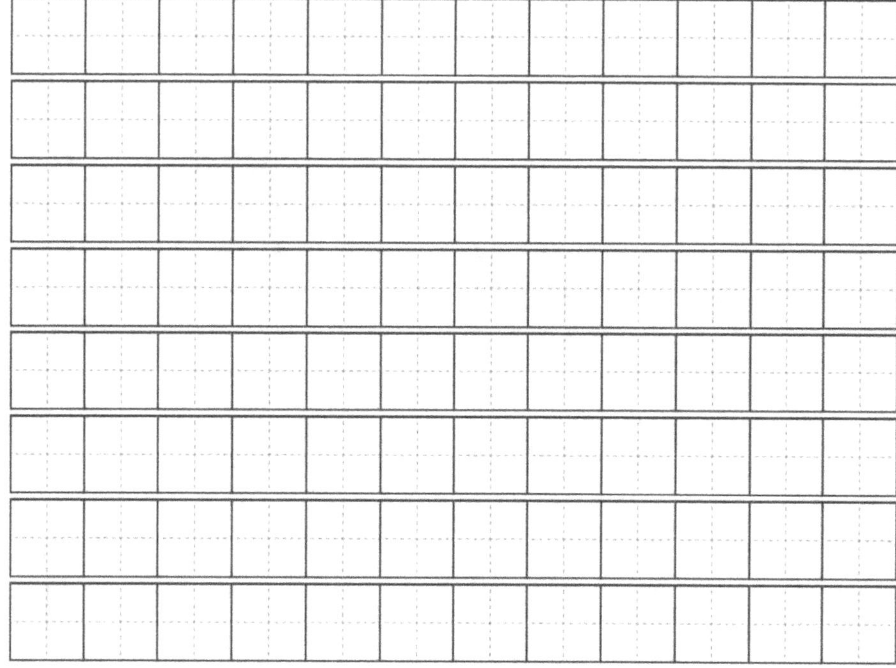

Match the Chinese words with the pictures.

☐ 电视	☐ 钱	☐ 出租车
☐ 苹果	☐ 吃	☐ 朋友们
☐ 飞机	☐ 衣服	☐ 狗
☐ 书	☐ 打电话	☐ 下雨
☐ 桌子	☐ 买	☐ 妈妈
☐ 电脑	☐ 医生	☐ 猫
☐ 喝	☐ 电影	☐ 医院

Write the pinyin into the squares.

Across		**Down**	
3 岁	33 学习	1 和	35 怎么
4 几	35 在	2 月	38 个
5 没关系	36 下雨	3 什么	39 水
7 来	37 朋友	4 家	41 我们
8 儿子	40 去	5 名字	44 九
9 女儿	41 五	6 星期	45 读
11 呢	42 没	7 六	46 少
12 不	43 茶	10 一	48 零
13 听	45 的	12 本	50 我
14 吗	47 妈妈	15 些	51 下
16 字	48 里	17 老师	52 爱
17 了	49 中午	18 猫	
18 明天	53 看见	19 年	
20 时	54 叫	20 上	
21 七		21 请	
22 他		23 多	
23 电影		24 衣服	
25 四		26 东西	
26 都		27 汉语	
27 很		28 对不起	
29 那		31 下午	
30 医院		33 写	
32 哪		34 学生	

REVISION
Crossword

Complete the crossword by entering the Pinyin of the supplied Chinese words.
This time, instead of providing you with clear indications as to where
the words should go, we show you hints of the tones in some of the squares.

airplane	__________	spot	__________
and	__________	sun, date	__________
Beijing	__________	table	__________
book	__________	taxi	__________
bye	__________	television	__________
to be able to	__________	thank you	__________
can; will	__________	this	__________
chair	__________	three	__________
China	__________	time	__________
cold	__________	to be; yes	__________
cup	__________	to buy	__________
dad	__________	to eat	__________
dish, vegetable	__________	to have	__________
dog	__________	to know, to be	__________
eight	__________	familiar with	
hello, hey	__________	to like	__________
hot	__________	to live, to reside	__________
how about	__________	to open	__________
in front	__________	to return	__________
miss, young lady	__________	to sit	__________
money	__________	today	__________
now	__________	too, excessively	__________
people	__________	weather	__________
piece	__________	work	__________
railway station	__________	yesterday	__________
restaurant	__________	you	__________

REVISION
Fill-in

Group the words according to their meaning.

八, 杯子, 北京, 吃, 电脑, 电视, 儿子, 饭馆, 好, 喝, 很, 火车站,
九, 老师, 冷, 零, 六, 女儿, 朋友, 七, 商店, 上午, 十, 书, 四, 同学,
五, 先生, 学生, 学校, 衣服, 医生, 医院, 椅子, 中国, 桌子, 昨天

Number	Location	People	Object	NONE

Part Two

UNIT 7
VOCABULARY

1.	一下儿	yíxiàr	one time, a little bit
2.	一半	yíbàn	half
3.	一边	yìbiān	one side, at the same time
4.	一会儿	yíhuìr	a little while
5.	一块儿	yíkuàir	the same place, together
6.	一些	yìxiē	some
7.	一点儿	yìdiǎnr	a little bit
8.	一起	yìqǐ	together
9.	一样	yíyàng	same, alike
10.	干	gàn	to do
11.	干	gān	dry
12.	干什么	gàn shénme	what to do
13.	干净	gānjìng	clean
14.	工人	gōngrén	worker
15.	下车	xià chē	to get off (a car)
16.	下班	xià//bān	to get off work
17.	大学	dàxué	university
18.	大学生	dàxuéshēng	university student
19.	上车	shàng chē	to get on (a car)
20.	上边	shàngbian	above; on; upper
21.	上网	shàng//wǎng	to go online
22.	上次	shàng cì	last time
23.	上学	shàng//xué	to go to school
24.	上班	shàng//bān	to go to work
25.	上课	shàng//kè	to have a class

Match the Hanzi with the corresponding Pinyin and English translation.

1.	一下儿	☐	dàxué	☐	a little bit
2.	一半	☐	dàxuéshēng	☐	a little while
3.	一边	☐	gàn	☐	above; on; upper
4.	一会儿	☐	gān	☐	clean
5.	一块儿	☐	gàn shénme	☐	dry
6.	一些	☐	gānjìng	☐	half
7.	一点儿	☐	gōngrén	☐	last time
8.	一起	☐	shàng//bān	☐	one side, at the same time
9.	一样	☐	shàngbian	☐	one time, a little bit
10.	干	☐	shàng chē	☐	same, alike
11.	干	☐	shàng cì	☐	some
12.	干什么	☐	shàng//kè	☐	the same place, together
13.	干净	☐	shàng//wǎng	☐	to have a class
14.	工人	☐	shàng//xué	☐	to do
15.	下车	☐	xià//bān	☐	to get off (a car)
16.	下班	☐	xià chē	☐	to get off work
17.	大学	☐	yíbàn	☐	to get on (a car)
18.	大学生	☐	yíkuàir	☐	to go online
19.	上车	☐	yíxiàr	☐	to go to school
20.	上边	☐	yìxiē	☐	to go to work
21.	上网	☐	yìbiān	☐	together
22.	上次	☐	yìdiǎnr	☐	university
23.	上学	☐	yíhuìr	☐	university student
24.	上班	☐	yìqǐ	☐	what to do
25.	上课	☐	yíyàng	☐	worker

Once ready, check your solution with the help of the previous page.

UNIT 7
Word search

Find the Chinese characters belonging to the following Pinyin words. In the grid, words with multiple characters can appear either vertically from top to bottom, or horizontally from left to right.

dàxué	gānjìng	shàngkè	xià chē	yìbiān
dàxuéshēng	gōngrén	shàngxué	yíbàn	yìdiǎnr
gàn	shàngbian	shàngbān	yíkuàir	yíhuìr
gān	shàng chē	shàngwǎng	yíxiàr	yìqǐ
gàn shénme	shàng cì	xiàbān	yìxiē	yíyàng

一	猫	大	漂	妈	妈	一	起	杯	子	一	样
下	能	学	亮	上	一	和	一	块	儿	医	来
儿	看	生	工	学	边	回	没	再	见	院	上
火	下	老	人	多	上	班	关	写	电	影	课
车	车	师	钱	干	北	这	系	哪	干	净	坐
站	的	出	租	车	京	今	一	些	苹	朋	大
大	学	是	一	会	儿	天	谁	狗	果	友	学
多	东	干	星	现	在	上	学	名	字	一	生
少	西	什	期	上	边	饭	馆	干	同	点	日
一	后	么	时	昨	天	我	上	衣	学	儿	叫
起	面	点	候	一	半	医	网	服	上	明	下
菜	字	上	车	汉	语	生	他	茶	次	天	班

A few Hanzi belonging to the Pinyin words above can be found twice in the grid. Take one of the pairs and insert them into the empty spaces below so that you get a meaningful sentence.

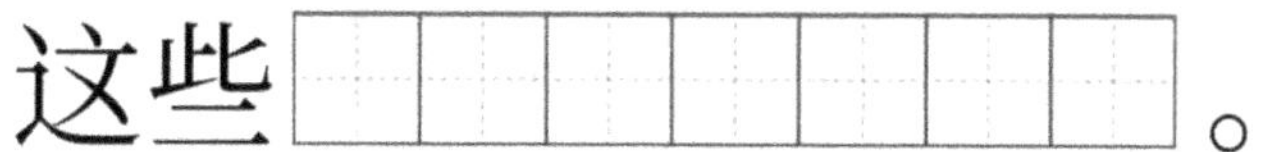

UNIT 7
Crossword

Put the English translation of the Chinese words into the squares. If the English translation contains more than one word, you must enter them without space into the squares.

Across

1 下班
5 上班
6 上
7 上课
8 一样
10 大学生
13 工人
15 上次
16 半
17 上车
18 一点儿

Down

1 上网
2 一边
3 干
4 一些
9 上学
11 一块儿
12 干
14 干净

UNIT 7
Fill-in

Complete the crossword by entering the Pinyin of the supplied Chinese words.
This time, instead of providing you with clear indications as to where
the words should go, we show you hints of the tones in some of the squares.

一下儿 ______

一半 ______

一边 ______

一会儿 ______

一块儿 ______

一些 ______

一点儿 ______

一起 ______

一样 ______

干 ______

干 ______

干净 ______

工人 ______

下车 ______

大学 ______

大学生 ______

上车 ______

上边 ______

上网 ______

上次 ______

上学 ______

上班 ______

上课 ______

Create words from the letters found in the letter cloud and
write them next to their English translation. You can use each letter only once.

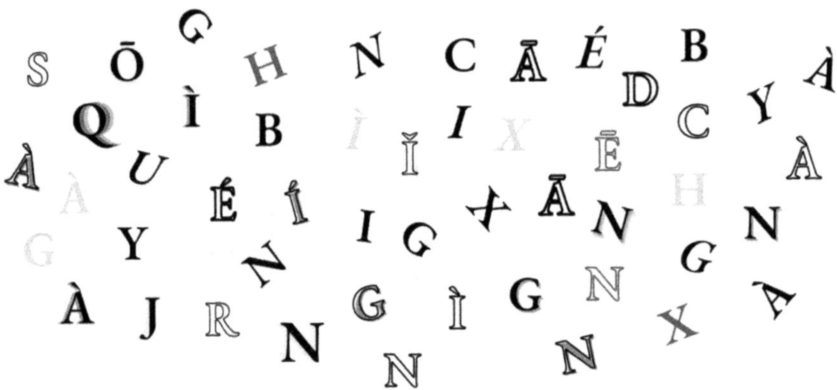

clean   _________________

half   _________________

last time   _________________

to get off a car _________________

to get off work _________________

together   _________________

university   _________________

worker   _________________

If you did a good job, by now there should be only three unused letters in the cloud.
Make a Pinyin word out of them and write down its English translation.

_____________   _____________________

1.	下边	xiàbian	below; under
2.	下次	xià cì	next time
3.	下课	xià//kè	to finish class
4.	小时	xiǎoshí	hour
5.	小朋友	xiǎopéngyǒu	child; kid
6.	小学	xiǎoxué	primary school
7.	小学生	xiǎoxuéshēng	elementary school student
8.	小孩儿	xiǎoháir	child; kid
9.	口	kǒu	mouth
10.	山	shān	mountain
11.	门	mén	door, gate
12.	门口	ménkǒu	doorway, treshold
13.	门票	ménpiào	tickets
14.	子	zi	noun suffix
15.	也	yě	also
16.	女	nǚ	woman, female
17.	女人	nǚrén	woman
18.	女生	nǚshēng	girl student
19.	女朋友	nǚpéngyou	girlfriend
20.	女孩儿	nǚháir	girl
21.	不	bù	no
22.	不大	bú dà	not big
23.	不用	búyòng	no need to
24.	不对	búduì	wrong, not correct
25.	车	chē	car

Match the Hanzi with the corresponding Pinyin and English translation.

#	Hanzi		Pinyin		English
1.	下边	☐	bù	☐	also
2.	下次	☐	bú dà	☐	below; under
3.	下课	☐	búduì	☐	car
4.	小时	☐	búyòng	☐	child; kid
5.	小朋友	☐	chē	☐	child; kid
6.	小学	☐	kǒu	☐	door, gate
7.	小学生	☐	mén	☐	doorway, treshold
8.	小孩儿	☐	ménkǒu	☐	elementary school student
9.	口	☐	ménpiào	☐	girl
10.	山	☐	nǔ	☐	girl student
11.	门	☐	nǔháir	☐	girlfriend
12.	门口	☐	nǔpéngyou	☐	hour
13.	门票	☐	nǔrén	☐	mountain
14.	子	☐	nǔshēng	☐	mouth
15.	也	☐	shān	☐	next time
16.	女	☐	xiàbian	☐	no
17.	女人	☐	xià cì	☐	no need to
18.	女生	☐	xià//kè	☐	not big
19.	女朋友	☐	xiǎoháir	☐	noun suffix
20.	女孩儿	☐	xiǎopéngyǒu	☐	primary school
21.	不	☐	xiǎoxué	☐	tickets
22.	不大	☐	xiǎoxuéshēng	☐	to finish class
23.	不用	☐	xiǎoshí	☐	woman, female
24.	不对	☐	yě	☐	woman
25.	车	☐	zi	☐	wrong, not correct

Once ready, check your solution with the help of the previous page.

Find the Chinese characters belonging to the following Pinyin words. In the grid, words with multiple characters can appear either vertically from top to bottom, or horizontally from left to right.

bù	kǒu	nǔháir	xiàbian	xiǎoxué
bú dà	mén	nǔpéngyou	xià cì	xiǎoxuéshēng
búduì	ménkǒu	nǔrén	xiàkè	xiǎoshí
búyòng	ménpiào	nǔshēng	xiǎoháir	yě
chē	nǔ	shān	xiǎopéngyǒu	zi

小	没	呢	饭	馆	明	不	狗	哪	口	星	期
朋	关	小	孩	儿	天	对	也	昨	天	都	女
友	系	高	兴	学	习	漂	茶	小	时	请	孩
冷	朋	怎	么	下	边	亮	女	爱	做	零	儿
不	友	山	菜	和	喝	家	生	睡	门	票	些
我	小	孩	儿	谁	门	谢	谢	觉	现	是	女
们	的	下	喜	猫	商	店	小	学	在	门	口
女	热	课	欢	车	杯	子	想	桌	下	读	看
人	工	苹	果	干	学	喂	女	子	次	椅	不
住	人	小	学	生	生	门	人	能	上	子	大
小	学	边	说	话	钱	口	坐	子	班	很	爸
一	半	女	朋	友	这	点	你	下	车	不	用

A few Hanzi belonging to the Pinyin words above can be found twice in the grid. Take one of the pairs and insert them into the empty spaces below so that you get a meaningful sentence.

这些☐☐和那些☐☐☐要在☐☐的☐☐见面。

Put the English translation of the Chinese words into the squares. If the English translation contains more than one word, you must enter them without space into the squares.

Across

1 不对

5 小时

7 不大

8 门票

10 女朋友

11 口

13 车

15 小学

16 也

17 下边

Down

1 女

2 不

3 山

4 下次

6 下课

9 门

12 女孩儿

14 小孩儿

Complete the crossword by entering the Pinyin of the supplied Chinese words.
This time, instead of providing you with clear indications as to where
the words should go, we show you hints of the tones in some of the squares.

下边 ______	山 ______	女生 ______
下次 ______	门 ______	女朋友 ______
下课 ______	门口 ______	女孩儿 ______
小时 ______	门票 ______	不 ______
小学生 ______	也 ______	不用 ______
小孩儿 ______	女 ______	不对 ______
口 ______	女人 ______	车 ______

Create words from the letters found in the letter cloud and
write them next to their English translation. You can use each letter only once.

also   __________________

car   __________________

hour   __________________

mountain   __________________

mouth   __________________

ticket   __________________

woman   __________________

wrong   __________________

If you did a good job, by now there should be only five unused letters in the cloud.
Make a Pinyin word out of them and write down its English translation!

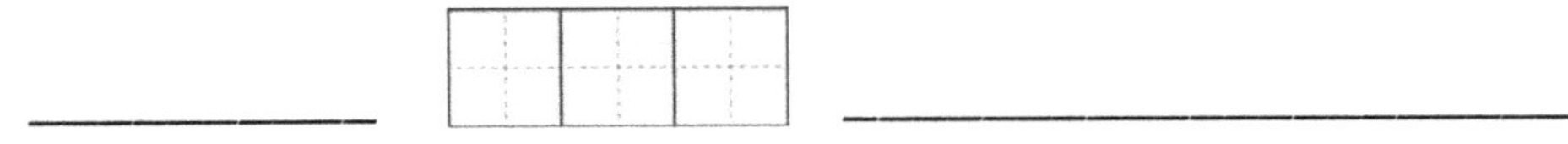

UNIT 9
VOCABULARY

1.	飞	fēi	to fly
2.	马上	mǎshàng	right now; right off
3.	马路	mǎlù	road; street
4.	开车	kāi//chē	to drive a car
5.	开会	kāi//huì	to have a meeting
6.	开玩笑	kāi wánxiào	to make fun of
7.	天	tiān	day
8.	元	yuán	Yuan; unit; element
9.	车上	chē shang	in the car
10.	车站	chēzhàn	station
11.	车票	chēpiào	ticket
12.	比	bǐ	particle used for comparison
13.	日期	rìqī	date
14.	中	zhōng	middle; in
15.	中文	Zhōngwén	Chinese
16.	中间	zhōngjiān	centre; between; middle
17.	中学	zhōngxué	middle school
18.	中学生	zhōngxuéshēng	middle school student
19.	见	jiàn	to see; to meet
20.	见面	jiàn//miàn	to meet
21.	午饭	wǔfàn	lunch
22.	手	shǒu	hand
23.	手机	shǒujī	mobile phone
24.	牛奶	niúnǎi	milk
25.	毛	máo	hair; unit of money

Match the Hanzi with the corresponding Pinyin and English translation.

#	Hanzi	Pinyin	English
1.	飞	☐ bǐ	☐ centre; between; middle
2.	马上	☐ chēpiào	☐ Chinese
3.	马路	☐ chē shang	☐ date
4.	开车	☐ chēzhàn	☐ day
5.	开会	☐ fēi	☐ hair; unit of money
6.	开玩笑	☐ jiàn	☐ hand
7.	天	☐ jiàn//miàn	☐ in the car
8.	元	☐ kāi//chē	☐ lunch
9.	车上	☐ kāi//huì	☐ middle school
10.	车站	☐ kāi wánxiào	☐ middle School student
11.	车票	☐ mǎlù	☐ middle; in
12.	比	☐ máo	☐ milk
13.	日期	☐ mǎshàng	☐ mobile phone
14.	中	☐ niúnǎi	☐ particle used for comparison
15.	中文	☐ rìqī	☐ right now; right off
16.	中间	☐ shǒu	☐ road; street
17.	中学	☐ shǒujī	☐ station
18.	中学生	☐ tiān	☐ ticket
19.	见	☐ wǔfàn	☐ to drive a car
20.	见面	☐ yuán	☐ to fly
21.	午饭	☐ zhōng	☐ to have a meeting
22.	手	☐ zhōngxué	☐ to make fun of
23.	手机	☐ zhōngxuéshēng	☐ to meet
24.	牛奶	☐ zhōngjiān	☐ to see; to meet
25.	毛	☐ Zhōngwén	☐ Yuan; unit; element

Once ready, check your solution with the help of the previous page.

Find the Chinese characters belonging to the following Pinyin words. In the grid, words with multiple characters can appear either vertically from top to bottom, or horizontally from left to right.

bǐ	jiàn	mǎlù	shǒu	zhōng
chēpiào	jiànmiàn	máo	shǒujī	zhōngxué
chē shang	kāichē	mǎshàng	tiān	zhōngxuéshēng
chēzhàn	kāihuì	niúnǎi	wǔfàn	zhōngjiān
fēi	kāi wánxiào	rìqī	yuán	Zhōngwén

椅	天	请	毛	怎	高	说	话	桌	子	看	漂
子	中	学	生	么	兴	开	车	零	中	间	亮
的	苹	果	飞	样	车	上	和	车	学	习	昨
中	听	名	字	会	吗	日	坐	票	现	手	天
住	车	午	饭	哪	茶	期	医	生	在	机	来
手	站	她	没	马	路	对	四	中	学	时	见
这	朋	牛	关	米	年	不	比	些	星	候	狗
吃	友	奶	系	饭	马	起	商	店	期	车	回
开	东	西	中	我	上	后	面	岁	他	站	老
会	再	见	学	们	先	水	开	玩	笑	点	师
喝	元	写	生	多	生	中	汉	语	见	喜	马
叫	同	学	衣	服	本	文	喂	月	面	欢	上

A few Hanzi belonging to the Pinyin words above can be found twice in the grid. Take one of the pairs and insert them into the empty spaces below so that you get a meaningful sentence.

这些老师和□□□□□□要去火□□。

Put the English translation of the Chinese words into the squares. If the English translation contains more than one word, you must enter them without space into the squares.

Across

1 马上

7 中

9 中学

10 日期

12 天

14 手机

16 午饭

17 车站

18 开车

Down

2 车上

3 开会

4 车票

5 飞

6 手

8 马路

11 见面

13 中文

15 元

Complete the crossword by entering the Pinyin of the supplied Chinese words.
This time, instead of providing you with clear indications as to where
the words should go, we show you hints of the tones in some of the squares.

飞　　______
马上　______
马路　______
开车　______
开会　______
天　　______
元　　______

车上　______
车站　______
车票　______
日期　______
中　　______
中文　______
中间　______

中学生　______
见　　______
见面　______
手机　______
牛奶　______
毛　　______

UNIT 9
Letter Cloud

Create Pinyin words from the letters found in the letter cloud and
write them next to their English translation. You can use each letter only once.

Chinese   _______________

date   _______________

day, heaven   _______________

mobile phone   _______________

ticket   _______________

to fly   _______________

to have a meeting   _______________

to meet   _______________

If you did a good job, by now there should be only four unused letters in the cloud.
Make a Pinyin word out of them and write down its English translation!

_______________   _______________

UNIT 10
VOCABULARY

1.	介绍	jièshào	to introduce
2.	从	cóng	from
3.	今年	jīnnián	this year
4.	分	fēn	to divide; minute
5.	风	fēng	wind
6.	火车	huǒchē	train
7.	认真	rènzhēn	conscientious
8.	书包	shūbāo	school bag
9.	书店	shūdiàn	bookstore
10.	打	dǎ	to hit, to take
11.	打开	dǎ//kāi	to turn on
12.	打车	dǎ//chē	to take a taxi
13.	打球	dǎ qiú	to play ball
14.	正	zhèng	straight; just; exactly
15.	正在	zhèngzài	in process of
16.	本子	běnzi	book
17.	东	dōng	east
18.	东边	dōngbian	east side
19.	北	běi	north
20.	北边	běibian	north side
21.	电	diàn	electricity
22.	电视机	diànshìjī	television
23.	电话	diànhuà	phone
24.	电影院	diànyǐngyuàn	cinema; movie theater
25.	别	bié	don't

Match the Hanzi with the corresponding Pinyin and English translation.

	Hanzi		Pinyin		English
1.	介绍	☐	běi	☐	book
2.	从	☐	běibian	☐	bookstore
3.	今年	☐	běnzi	☐	cinema; movie theater
4.	分	☐	bié	☐	conscientious
5.	风	☐	cóng	☐	don't
6.	火车	☐	dǎ	☐	east
7.	认真	☐	dǎ//chē	☐	east side
8.	书包	☐	dǎ//kāi	☐	electricity
9.	书店	☐	dǎ qiú	☐	from
10.	打	☐	diàn	☐	in process of
11.	打开	☐	diànhuà	☐	north
12.	打车	☐	diànshìjī	☐	north side
13.	打球	☐	diànyǐngyuàn	☐	phone
14.	正	☐	dōng	☐	school bag
15.	正在	☐	dōngbian	☐	straight; just; exactly
16.	本子	☐	fēn	☐	television
17.	东	☐	fēng	☐	this year
18.	东边	☐	huǒchē	☐	to divide; minute
19.	北	☐	jièshào	☐	to hit, to take
20.	北边	☐	jīnnián	☐	to introduce
21.	电	☐	rènzhēn	☐	to play ball
22.	电视机	☐	shūbāo	☐	to take a taxi
23.	电话	☐	shūdiàn	☐	to turn on
24.	电影院	☐	zhèng	☐	train
25.	别	☐	zhèngzài	☐	wind

Once ready, check your solution with the help of the previous page.

UNIT 10
Word search

Find the Chinese characters belonging to the following Pinyin words. In the grid, words with multiple characters can appear either vertically from top to bottom, or horizontally from left to right.

běi	dǎ	diànhuà	fēn	rènzhēn
běibian	dǎchē	diànshìjī	fēng	shūbāo
běnzi	dǎkāi	diànyǐngyuàn	huǒchē	shūdiàn
bié	dǎ qiú	dōng	jièshào	zhèng
cóng	diàn	dōngbian	jīnnián	zhèngzài

前 从 饭 馆 哪 有 狗 现 高 兴 呢 正
面 时 看 打 来 打 苹 在 北 你 后 面
点 候 坐 车 学 她 果 米 昨 今 没 别
先 火 朋 友 生 介 绍 饭 天 年 冷 同
生 车 和 电 医 生 学 打 车 好 毛 学
东 些 里 视 买 打 习 星 北 爸 本 子
杯 听 日 机 手 开 我 期 边 我 们 衣
子 分 期 是 明 都 正 在 医 书 包 服
电 手 认 真 天 电 学 风 院 茶 块 没
影 机 名 字 爱 话 校 这 电 中 正 关
院 书 吗 东 边 住 打 中 影 学 在 系
字 店 的 牛 奶 岁 球 文 院 马 路 电

A few Hanzi belonging to the Pinyin words above can be found twice in the grid. Take one of the pairs and insert them into the empty spaces below so that you get a meaningful sentence.

我的弟弟　□□□□，他要去□□□。

UNIT 10
Crossword

Put the English translation of the Chinese words into the squares. If the English translation contains more than one word, you must enter them without space into the squares.

Across

1 风
5 电话
7 打开
8 打车
9 北
10 书店
12 电视机
13 正
15 认真

Down

2 别
3 电影院
4 分
5 打球
6 电
7 火车
8 今年
10 本子
11 从
14 打

UNIT 10
Fill-in

Complete the crossword by entering the Pinyin of the supplied Chinese words.
This time, instead of providing you with clear indications as to where
the words should go, we show you hints of the tones in some of the squares.

从 _______

分 _______

风 _______

打 _______

东 _______

北 _______

别 _______

介绍 _______

今年 _______

火车 _______

认真 _______

书包 _______

书店 _______

打开 _______

打车 _______

打球 _______

正在 _______

本子 _______

东边 _______

北边 _______

电视机 _______

电话 _______

Create Pinyin words from the letters found in the letter cloud and
write them next to their English translation. You can use each letter only once.

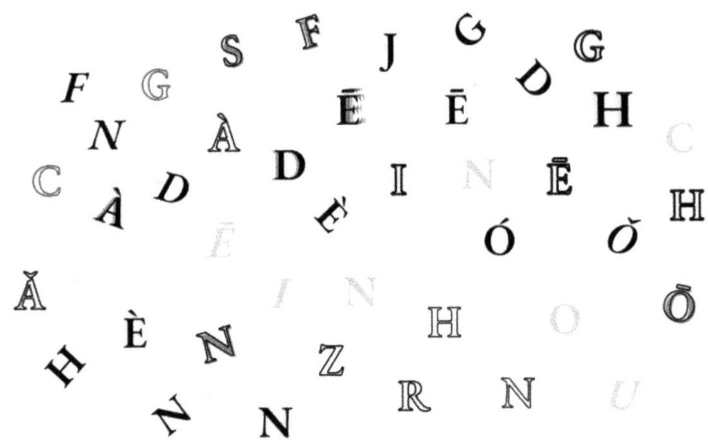

conscientious   _______________________

east   _______________________

from   _______________________

to divide   _______________________

to hit   _______________________

to introduce   _______________________

train   _______________________

wind   _______________________

If you did a good job, by now there should be only four unused letters in the cloud.
Make a Pinyin word out of them and write down its English translation!

_______________   _______________________

UNIT 11
VOCABULARY

1.	去年	qùnián	last year
2.	左	zuǒ	left
3.	左边	zuǒbian	left side
4.	右	yòu	right
5.	右边	yòubian	right side
6.	号	hào	number; date
7.	生日	shēngrì	birthday
8.	生气	shēng//qì	to get angry
9.	生病	shēng//bìng	to fall ill
10.	们	men	plural marker
11.	白	bái	white
12.	白天	báitiān	day, daytime
13.	他们	tāmen	they
14.	用	yòng	to use
15.	外	wài	outside, abroad
16.	外边	wàibian	outside, exterior
17.	外国	wàiguó	foreign country
18.	外语	wàiyǔ	foreign language
19.	包	bāo	bag
20.	包子	bāozi	bun
21.	半	bàn	half
22.	半天	bàntiān	half day
23.	半年	bàn nián	half a year
24.	出	chū	to (go/come) out
25.	出来	chū//•lái	to come out

Match the Hanzi with the corresponding Pinyin and English translation.

	Hanzi		Pinyin		English
1.	去年	☐	bái	☐	bag
2.	左	☐	báitiān	☐	birthday
3.	左边	☐	bàn	☐	bun
4.	右	☐	bàn nián	☐	day, daytime
5.	右边	☐	bàntiān	☐	foreign country
6.	号	☐	bāo	☐	foreign language
7.	生日	☐	bāozi	☐	half
8.	生气	☐	chū	☐	half a year
9.	生病	☐	chū//•lái	☐	half day
10.	们	☐	hào	☐	last year
11.	白	☐	men	☐	left
12.	白天	☐	qùnián	☐	left side
13.	他们	☐	shēng//bìng	☐	number; date
14.	用	☐	shēng//qì	☐	outside, abroad
15.	外	☐	shēngrì	☐	outside, exterior
16.	外边	☐	tāmen	☐	plural marker
17.	外国	☐	wài	☐	right
18.	外语	☐	wàibian	☐	right side
19.	包	☐	wàiguó	☐	they
20.	包子	☐	wàiyǔ	☐	to (go/come) out
21.	半	☐	yòng	☐	to come out
22.	半天	☐	yòu	☐	to fall ill
23.	半年	☐	yòubian	☐	to get angry
24.	出	☐	zuǒ	☐	to use
25.	出来	☐	zuǒbian	☐	white

Once ready, check your solution with the help of the previous page.

UNIT 11
Word search

Find the Chinese characters belonging to the following Pinyin words. In the grid, words with multiple characters can appear either vertically from top to bottom, or horizontally from left to right.

bái	bāo	men	tāmen	yòng
báitiān	bāozi	qùnián	wài	yòu
bàn	chū	shēngbìng	wàibian	yòubian
bàn nián	chūlái	shēngqì	wàiguó	zuǒ
bàntiān	hào	shēngrì	wàiyǔ	zuǒbian

一	说	话	生	北	前	面	日	外	叫	喜	号
边	包	月	气	京	水	去	年	天	气	欢	六
多	他	中	认	飞	机	女	少	外	语	电	们
左	边	午	识	外	谁	儿	半	下	开	视	书
工	很	生	病	时	候	右	商	雨	白	天	家
人	白	分	钟	出	写	边	店	漂	四	对	的
会	太	出	外	东	做	喝	去	亮	五	不	出
火	生	租	国	西	电	影	年	生	病	起	来
车	日	车	三	他	们	后	面	小	姐	今	水
站	国	不	客	气	汉	左	昨	外	边	天	果
半	干	用	桌	子	语	去	天	睡	觉	哪	右
天	老	师	怎	么	包	子	看	半	年	朋	友

A few Hanzi belonging to the Pinyin words above can be found twice in the grid. Take one of the pairs and insert them into the empty spaces below so that you get a meaningful sentence.

UNIT 11
Crossword

Put the English translation of the Chinese words into the squares. If the English translation contains more than one word, you must enter them without space into the squares.

Across

2 半
4 左边
6 右
7 他们
8 半天
10 生气
11 包子
15 白天
16 用
18 外语

Down

1 生日
3 外
4 去年
5 外国
9 号
12 白
13 外边
14 生病
17 包

UNIT 11
Fill-in

Complete the crossword by entering the Pinyin of the supplied Chinese words.
This time, instead of providing you with clear indications as to where
the words should go, we show you hints of the tones in some of the squares.

去年 ______   外语 ______

左边 ______   白 ______   包 ______

右边 ______   白天 ______   包子 ______

号 ______   他们 ______   半 ______

生日 ______   用 ______   半天 ______

生气 ______   外 ______   半年 ______

生病 ______   外边 ______   出 ______

们 ______   外国 ______   出来 ______

UNIT 11
QUIZ

Choose the correct answer.

1. *To get angry* is

    a. shēngqì   b. shēngqí   c. shéngqí   d. shèngqì

2. *Outside* is

    a. wāibiān   b. wáibián   c. wàibian   d. wàibiàn

3. *To use* is

    a. yōng   b. yóng   c. yòng   d. yǒng

4. *Last year* is

    a. qúnián   b. qúniàn   c. qūniàn   d. qùnián

5. *Birthday* is

    a. shéngrì   b. shēngrì   c. shéngrí   d. shēngrí

6. *Daytime* is

    a. báitiān   b. báitián   c. bāitiān   d. bāitián

7. *Right* is

    a. yōu   b. yóu   c. yǒu   d. yòu

8. *Number/date* is

    a. háo   b. hào   c. hǎo   d. hāo

9. *Foreign country* is

    a. wáiguó   b. wàiguǒ   c. wāiguǒ   d. wàiguó

10. *Foreign language* is

    a. wáiyǔ   b. wàiyú   c. wàiyǔ   d. wāiyū

REVISION
Characters

Create Chinese characters from the components.

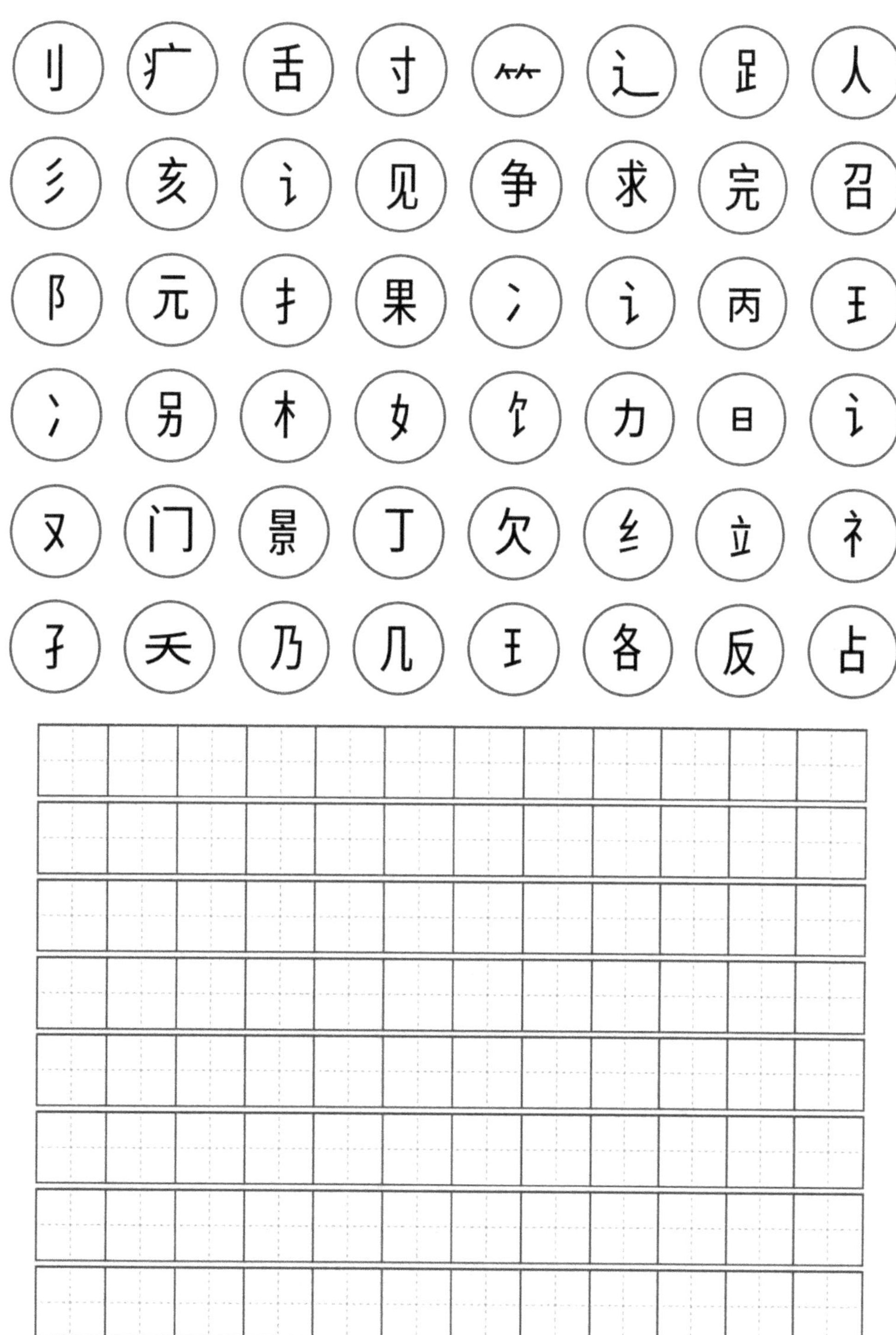

MILK
BOOKSTORE

Match the Chinese words with the pictures.

☐ 工人   ☐ 马路   ☐ 书包
☐ 口   ☐ 开会   ☐ 书店
☐ 山   ☐ 车   ☐ 打球
☐ 门口   ☐ 车站   ☐ 本子
☐ 女   ☐ 手   ☐ 电视机
☐ 女孩儿   ☐ 手机   ☐ 包
☐ 飞   ☐ 牛奶   ☐ 包子

Put the pinyin into the squares.

Across

1 中间
5 今年
7 上班
9 火车
11 马路
12 左
13 女人
15 分
17 打
18 别
19 马上
23 下班
24 认真
25 北
26 也
27 用
28 干
31 正
32 门票
34 电
35 打开
36 女
39 从
41 东边
42 大学
44 不大
45 包
47 中文
48 山
49 门
50 外语
51 天

Down

2 号
3 见面
4 去年
5 见
6 女生
7 手
8 非
10 车站
14 日期
16 电影院
17 打车
20 生气
21 干净
22 风
23 下次
27 一点儿
29 出
30 外国
32 门口
33 半
34 东
35 电话
37 工人
38 小时
40 牛奶
43 外
45 不
46 干

Put the pinyin into the squares.

REVISION
Fill in

Complete the crossword by entering the Pinyin of the supplied Chinese words.
This time, instead of providing you with clear indications as to where
the words should go, we show you hints of the tones in some of the squares.

一下儿	__________	一边	__________
一半	__________	一会儿	__________
一块儿	__________	一样	__________
一些	__________	上边	__________
一起	__________	上次	__________
下车	__________	上学	__________
下课	__________	小学	__________
小朋友	__________	小学生	__________
口	__________	小孩儿	__________
开车	__________	女孩儿	__________
开玩笑	__________	开会	__________
不用	__________	元	__________
中学生	__________	不对	__________
毛	__________	车票	__________
书店	__________	比	__________
正在	__________	中学	__________
本子	__________	午饭	__________
右	__________	介绍	__________
北边	__________	书包	__________
电视机	__________	打球	__________
生气	__________	生日	__________
白	__________	他们	__________
白天	__________	包子	__________
出来	__________	半年	__________

REVISION
Fill in

Put the pinyin into the squares.

REVISION
Group the Words

Group the words according to their meaning.

一会儿, 一块儿, 工人, 大学生, 小时, 小孩儿, 女朋友, 马上,
车票, 日期, 中间, 中学生, 手机, 今年, 风, 打球, 去年, 本子, 左,
右边, 北边, 电视机, 生气, 生病, 外语, 包, 半天, 出来

Time	Location	People	Object	NONE

UNIT 12
VOCABULARY

1.	汉字	Hànzì	Chinese character
2.	记	jì	to remember
3.	记住	jìzhù	to remember; to keep in mind
4.	记得	jìde	to remember, to recall
5.	出去	chū//•qù	to go out
6.	奶	nǎi	milk
7.	奶奶	nǎinai	grandma
8.	对	duì	correct/right
9.	动	dòng	to move
10.	动作	dòngzuò	movement, action
11.	考	kǎo	to test; to examine
12.	考试	kǎo//shì	examination
13.	老	lǎo	old; aged
14.	老人	lǎorén	old people; the aged
15.	地	de	aux. word after an adverbial phrase
16.	地	dì	earth, ground
17.	地上	dìshang	on the ground
18.	地方	dìfang	place, space, room
19.	地图	dìtú	map
20.	地点	dìdiǎn	place, location
21.	机场	jīchǎng	airport
22.	机票	jīpiào	air ticket
23.	过	guò	to go through, to spend time
24.	西	xī	west
25.	西边	xībian	west side

UNIT 12
Matching exercise

Match the Hanzi with the corresponding Pinyin and English translation.

#	Hanzi		Pinyin		English
1.	汉字	☐	chū//•qù	☐	air ticket
2.	记	☐	de	☐	airport
3.	记住	☐	dì	☐	aux. word after an adverbial phrase
4.	记得	☐	dìdiǎn	☐	Chinese character
5.	出去	☐	dìfang	☐	correct/right
6.	奶	☐	dìshang	☐	earth, ground
7.	奶奶	☐	dìtú	☐	examination
8.	对	☐	dòng	☐	grandma
9.	动	☐	dòngzuò	☐	map
10.	动作	☐	duì	☐	milk
11.	考	☐	guò	☐	movement, action
12.	考试	☐	Hànzì	☐	old people; the aged
13.	老	☐	jì	☐	old; aged
14.	老人	☐	jīchǎng	☐	on the ground
15.	地	☐	jìde	☐	place, location
16.	地	☐	jīpiào	☐	place, space, room
17.	地上	☐	jìzhù	☐	to go out
18.	地方	☐	kǎo	☐	to go through, to spend time
19.	地图	☐	kǎo//shì	☐	to move
20.	地点	☐	lǎo	☐	to remember
21.	机场	☐	lǎorén	☐	to remember, to recall
22.	机票	☐	nǎi	☐	to remember; to keep in mind
23.	过	☐	nǎinai	☐	to test; to examine
24.	西	☐	xī	☐	west
25.	西边	☐	xībian	☐	west side

Once ready, check your solution with the help of the previous page.

UNIT 12
Word search

Find the Chinese characters belonging to the following Pinyin words. In the grid, words with multiple characters can appear either vertically from top to bottom, or horizontally from left to right.

chūqù	dìshang	guò	jīpiào	lǎorén
de	dìtú	Hànzì	jìzhù	nǎi
dì	dòng	jì	kǎo	nǎinai
dìdiǎn	dòngzuò	jīchǎng	kǎoshì	xī
dìfang	duì	jìdé	lǎo	xībian

过	认	真	地	图	开	车	对	猫	西	大	能
爸	奶	现	在	上	地	开	玩	笑	边	学	动
爸	坐	学	生	次	衣	服	考	试	车	上	作
茶	老	人	些	汉	字	一	会	儿	记	没	狗
桌	子	来	这	时	候	星	再	见	得	关	高
明	记	住	不	机	医	期	地	苹	果	系	兴
天	饭	馆	对	票	生	在	点	昨	听	地	睡
动	吃	机	场	毛	地	好	电	天	呢	方	觉
米	我	名	字	上	网	学	视	水	老	马	考
饭	们	奶	出	租	车	习	出	果	岁	上	试
地	天	奶	有	考	干	我	去	电	西	杯	子
上	气	中	学	生	地	点	零	脑	妈	妈	记

A few Hanzi belonging to the Pinyin words above can be found twice in the grid. Take one of the pairs and insert them into the empty spaces below so that you get a meaningful sentence.

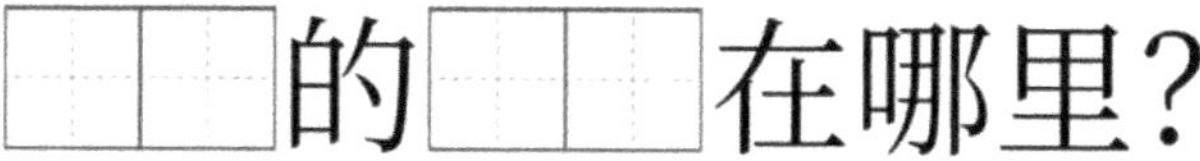

UNIT 12
Crossword

Put the English translation of the Chinese words into the squares. If the English translation contains more than one word, you must enter them without space into the squares.

<table>
<tr><td>

Across

3 对	13 动作
6 动	15 地图
8 过	16 奶奶
9 奶	17 机场
12 老	18 老人

</td><td>

Down

1 出去	10 地点
2 西边	11 考试
4 地上	12 机票
5 记	14 考
7 记得	

</td></tr>
</table>

UNIT 12
Fill-in

Complete the crossword by entering the Pinyin of the supplied Chinese words.
This time, instead of providing you with clear indications as to where
the words should go, we show you hints of the tones in some of the squares.

汉字 _________
记住 _________
记得 _________
出去 _________
奶 _________
奶奶 _________
对 _________
动 _________

动作 _________
考 _________
考试 _________
老人 _________
地 _________
地 _________
地上 _________

地方 _________
地图 _________
地点 _________
机场 _________
机票 _________
过 _________
西 _________
西边 _________

UNIT 12
QUIZ

Choose the correct answer.

1. *Movement* is

a. dóngzuó   b. dòngzuò   c. dōngzuò   d. dòngzuō

2. *To go out* is

a. chùqù   b. chúqù   c. chùqū   d. chūqù

3. *Grandma* is

a. nǎinai   b. náinai   c. nǎinái   d. nainǎi

4. *Place/location* is

a. dídiǎn   b. dǐdiǎn   c. dìdiǎn   d. dìdiān

5. *Air ticket* is

a. jīpiáo   b. jīpiào   c. jìpiào   d. jìpiǎo

6. *Examination* is

a. kǎoshì   b. kāoshì   c. kǎoshí   d. kāoshí

7. *Map* is

a. dítú   b. dítū   c. dìtǔ   d. dìtú

8. *Airport* is

a. jìcháng   b. jīchǎng   c. jìchǎng   d. jīchāng

9. *West side* is

a. xìbiǎn   b. xībiǎn   c. xībian   d. xìbián

10. *To pass time* is

a. guǒ   b. guō   c. guò   d. guó

UNIT 13
VOCABULARY

1.	再	zài	again
2.	在家	zàijiā	at home
3.	有些	yǒuxiē	some; somewhat
4.	有用	yǒuyòng	useful
5.	有名	yǒu//míng	famous
6.	有时候	yǒushíhou	sometimes
7.	有的	yǒude	some
8.	百	bǎi	hundred
9.	页	yè	page
10.	早	zǎo	early
11.	早上	zǎoshang	morning
12.	早饭	zǎofàn	breakfast
13.	吃饭	chī//fàn	to have meal
14.	回去	huí//•qù	to go back
15.	回来	huí//•lái	to come back; to return
16.	回到	huídào	to go back to
17.	回家	huí jiā	to go home
18.	回答	huídá	answer
19.	网上	wǎng shang	online
20.	肉	ròu	meat
21.	后	hòu	back; behind; after; later
22.	后天	hòutiān	day after tomorrow
23.	后边	hòubian	behind; back
24.	次	cì	second-rate; measure word
25.	关	guān	to shut; to close

Match the Hanzi with the corresponding Pinyin and English translation.

#	Hanzi		Pinyin		English
1.	再	☐	bǎi	☐	again
2.	在家	☐	chī//fàn	☐	answer
3.	有些	☐	cì	☐	at home
4.	有用	☐	guān	☐	back; behind; after; later
5.	有名	☐	hòu	☐	behind; back
6.	有时候	☐	hòubian	☐	breakfast
7.	有的	☐	hòutiān	☐	day after tomorrow
8.	百	☐	huídá	☐	early
9.	页	☐	huídào	☐	famous
10.	早	☐	huí jiā	☐	hundred
11.	早上	☐	huí//•lái	☐	meat
12.	早饭	☐	huí//•qù	☐	morning
13.	吃饭	☐	ròu	☐	online
14.	回去	☐	wǎng shang	☐	page
15.	回来	☐	yè	☐	second-rate; measure word
16.	回到	☐	yǒude	☐	some
17.	回家	☐	yǒu//míng	☐	some; somewhat
18.	回答	☐	yǒushíhou	☐	sometimes
19.	网上	☐	yǒuxiē	☐	to come back; to return
20.	肉	☐	yǒuyòng	☐	to go back
21.	后	☐	zài	☐	to go back to
22.	后天	☐	zàijiā	☐	to go home
23.	后边	☐	zǎo	☐	to have meal
24.	次	☐	zǎofàn	☐	to shut; to close
25.	关	☐	zǎoshang	☐	useful

Once ready, check your solution with the help of the previous page.

UNIT 13
Word search

Find the Chinese characters belonging to the following Pinyin words. In the grid, words with multiple characters can appear either vertically from top to bottom, or horizontally from left to right.

bǎi	hòubian	huílái	yǒude	zài
chīfàn	hòutiān	huíqù	yǒumíng	zàijiā
cì	huídá	ròu	yǒushíhou	zǎo
guān	huídào	wǎng shang	yǒuxiē	zǎofàn
hòu	huí jiā	yè	yǒuyòng	zǎoshang

记	回	书	早	山	出	奶	奶	早	上	记	百
得	到	包	今	后	来	有	名	口	地	吃	车
不	介	绍	年	天	中	学	飞	早	图	饭	上
大	有	时	候	打	回	女	手	饭	小	手	网
小	时	天	元	开	去	孩	有	认	学	机	上
也	页	号	开	有	北	儿	的	真	生	午	饭
肉	马	后	玩	用	边	后	动	作	早	上	见
外	上	半	笑	火	车	边	正	在	机	打	在
吃	饭	马	路	回	去	风	回	来	票	车	家
见	面	在	车	答	年	再	日	期	生	回	电
生	日	家	站	朋	友	们	有	些	气	家	视
关	电	影	院	次	西	白	天	本	子	用	机

A few Hanzi belonging to the Pinyin words above can be found twice in the grid. Take one of the pairs and insert them into the empty spaces below so that you get a meaningful sentence.

101

UNIT 13
Crossword

Put the English translation of the Chinese words into the squares. If the English translation contains more than one word, you must enter them without space into the squares.

Across

2 回答
4 早
6 关
8 有名
9 有些
11 后边
12 吃饭
14 在家
16 有时候
17 肉
18 再

Down

1 回去
3 回来
5 回家
7 有用
10 网上
11 早饭
12 百
13 早上
15 页

Complete the crossword by entering the Pinyin of the supplied Chinese words.
This time, instead of providing you with clear indications as to where
the words should go, we show you hints of the tones in some of the squares.

在家 _______	早 _______	回答 _______
有用 _______	早上 _______	网上 _______
有名 _______	早饭 _______	肉 _______
有时候 _______	吃饭 _______	后天 _______
有的 _______	回去 _______	后边 _______
百 _______	回到 _______	次 _______
页 _______	回家 _______	关 _______

UNIT 13
QUIZ

Choose the correct answer.

1. *Again* is

    a. zái   b. zāi   c. zài   d. zǎi

2. *To have meal* is

    a. chífàn   b. chīfàn   c. chīfán   d. chífán

3. *To go back to* is

    a. huǐdào   b. huídāo   c. huǐdāo   d. huídào

4. *Hundred* is

    a. bāi   b. bái   c. bǎi   d. bài

5. *Page* is

    a. yè   b. yě   c. yé   d. yē

6. *Some/somewhat* is

    a. yōuxiē   b. yǒuxiě   c. yǒuxiē   d. yōuxiè

7. *At home* is

    a. záijià   b. zàijiā   c. zàijià   d. zāijià

8. *Useful* is

    a. yóuyòng   b. yǒuyóng   c. yǒuyòng   d. yóuyǒng

9. *Breakfast* is

    a. zǎofàn   b. zāofàn   c. záofàn   d. zāofǎn

10. *Famous* is

    a. yóumìng   b. yǒumìng   c. yōumīng   d. yǒumíng

UNIT 14
VOCABULARY

1.	网友	wǎngyǒu	net friend
2.	先	xiān	before; first
3.	休息	xiūxi	to rest
4.	行	xíng	that's ok
5.	爷爷	yéye	grandpa
6.	问	wèn	to ask
7.	关上	guānshang	to close; to turn off (light)
8.	忙	máng	busy
9.	那儿	nàr	there
10.	那边	nàbiān	over there
11.	那里	nà•lǐ	that place, there
12.	那些	nàxiē	those
13.	好吃	hǎochī	delicious
14.	好听	hǎotīng	pleasant to hear
15.	好玩儿	hǎowánr	fun; interesting
16.	好看	hǎokàn	good looking
17.	她们	tāmen	they
18.	进	jìn	to enter
19.	进去	jìn//•qù	to go in
20.	进来	jìn//•lái	to come in
21.	远	yuǎn	far
22.	花	huā	flower
23.	还	hái	also; still; yet
24.	还有	hái yǒu	also; in addition; besides
25.	还是	háishi	still; or

Match the Hanzi with the corresponding Pinyin and English translation.

#	Hanzi	Pinyin	English
1.	网友	☐ guānshang	☐ also; in addition; besides
2.	先	☐ hái	☐ also; still; yet
3.	休息	☐ háishi	☐ before; first
4.	行	☐ hái yǒu	☐ busy
5.	爷爷	☐ hǎochī	☐ delicious
6.	问	☐ hǎokàn	☐ far
7.	关上	☐ hǎotīng	☐ flower
8.	忙	☐ hǎowánr	☐ fun; interesting
9.	那儿	☐ huā	☐ good looking
10.	那边	☐ jìn	☐ grandpa
11.	那里	☐ jìn//•lái	☐ net friend
12.	那些	☐ jìn//•qù	☐ over there
13.	好吃	☐ máng	☐ pleasant to hear
14.	好听	☐ nàbiān	☐ still; or
15.	好玩儿	☐ nà•lǐ	☐ that place, there
16.	好看	☐ nàr	☐ that's ok
17.	她们	☐ nàxiē	☐ there
18.	进	☐ tāmen	☐ they
19.	进去	☐ wǎngyǒu	☐ those
20.	进来	☐ wèn	☐ to ask
21.	远	☐ xiān	☐ to close; to turn off (light)
22.	花	☐ xíng	☐ to come in
23.	还	☐ xiūxi	☐ to enter
24.	还有	☐ yéye	☐ to go in
25.	还是	☐ yuǎn	☐ to rest

Once ready, check your solution with the help of the previous page.

UNIT 14
Word search

Find the Chinese characters belonging to the following Pinyin words. In the grid, words with multiple characters can appear either vertically from top to bottom, or horizontally from left to right.

guānshang	hǎokàn	jìnlái	nàr	xiān
hái	hǎotīng	jìnqù	nàxiē	xíng
háishi	hǎowánr	máng	tāmen	xiūxi
hái yǒu	huā	nàbiān	wǎngyǒu	yéye
hǎochī	jìn	nàlǐ	wèn	yuǎn

白	北	边	关	车	出	去	进	奶	奶	考	试
天	对	认	上	站	还	有	介	好	火	那	边
机	休	真	半	西	记	手	绍	看	车	生	病
场	息	记	进	去	得	网	友	包	子	东	地
中	间	住	百	车	休	手	白	远	左	爷	方
生	日	好	正	票	息	机	花	号	边	爷	本
问	风	听	在	先	书	行	早	吃	还	今	子
去	忙	机	那	肉	店	再	那	饭	是	年	她
年	页	票	里	见	面	元	儿	日	期	毛	们
好	吃	比	山	动	好	下	车	下	那	些	也
老	马	进	来	生	玩	开	会	次	上	一	起
别	上	门	口	气	儿	左	爷	爷	班	分	还

A few Hanzi belonging to the Pinyin words above can be found twice in the grid. Take one of the pairs and insert them into the empty spaces below so that you get a meaningful sentence.

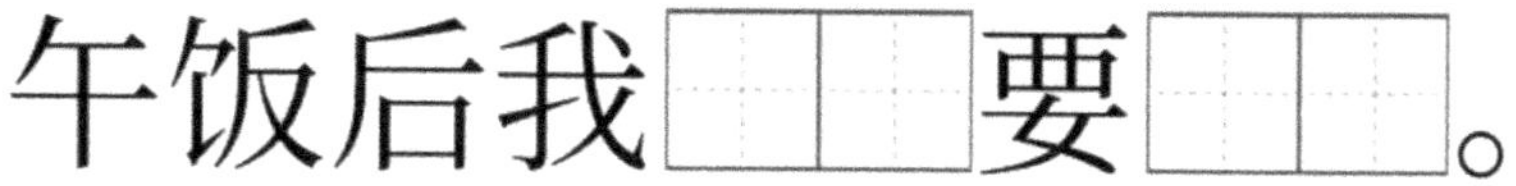

Put the English translation of the Chinese words into the squares. If the English translation contains more than one word, you must enter them without space into the squares.

Across

2 忙
7 好玩儿
11 她们
12 还有
14 那边
15 进来
16 网友
18 问
19 爷爷

Down

1 关上
3 还是
4 先
5 进去
6 花
8 那儿
9 好看
10 好吃
11 那些
13 休息
17 远

Complete the crossword by entering the Pinyin of the supplied Chinese words.
This time, instead of providing you with clear indications as to where
the words should go, we show you hints of the tones in some of the squares.

先 ______
行 ______
问 ______
忙 ______
远 ______
花 ______
还 ______
近 ______

网友 ______
休息 ______
爷爷 ______
关上 ______
那儿 ______
那边 ______

那里 ______
那些 ______
好吃 ______
好听 ______
好玩儿 ______
好看 ______

她们 ______
进去 ______
进来 ______
还有 ______
还是 ______

UNIT 14
QUIZ

Choose the correct answer.

1. *Delicious* is

    a. háochí   b. hāochī   c. hāochì   d. hǎochī

2. *Far* is

    a. yuàn   b. yuǎn   c. yuán   d. yuān

3. *To come in* is

    a. jínlái   b. jǐnlāi   c. jìnlái   d. jīnlái

4. *Busy* is

    a. māng   b. máng   c. mǎng   d. màng

5. *To rest* is

    a. xiūxi   b. xiúxi   c. xiūxí   d. xiùxí

6. *To close/to shut* is

    a. guānshang   b. guānshāng   c. guánshàng   d. guǎnshāng

7. *They* is

    a. támen   b. tǎmen   c. tàmen   d. tāmen

8. *Flower* is

    a. huá   b. huà   c. huā   d. huǎ

9. *To ask* is

    a. wèn   b. wěn   c. wēn   d. wén

10. *There* is

    a. nǎr   b. nár   c. nàr   d. nār

110

UNIT 15
VOCABULARY

1.	坏	huài	bad
2.	找	zhǎo	to look for
3.	找到	zhǎodào	to find
4.	走	zǒu	to go, to walk
5.	走路	zǒu//lù	to walk
6.	两	liǎng	two, both
7.	还	huán	to return; to pay back
8.	来到	láidào	to arrive
9.	时间	shíjiān	time
10.	里边	lǐbian	inside
11.	男	nán	man
12.	男人	nánrén	man
13.	男生	nánshēng	schoolboy
14.	男朋友	nánpéngyou	boyfriend
15.	男孩儿	nánháir	boy
16.	听见	tīng//jiàn	to hear
17.	听写	tīngxiě	dictation; to dictate
18.	听到	tīngdào	to hear
19.	吧	ba	interjection particle
20.	别人	bié•rén	other people
21.	别的	biéde	other
22.	告诉	gàosu	to tell
23.	你们	nǐmen	you (Pl.)
24.	身上	shēnshang	on one's body
25.	身体	shēntǐ	body

Match the Hanzi with the corresponding Pinyin and English translation.

#	Hanzi		Pinyin		English
1.	坏	☐	ba	☐	bad
2.	找	☐	biéde	☐	body
3.	找到	☐	bié•rén	☐	boy
4.	走	☐	gàosu	☐	boyfriend
5.	走路	☐	huài	☐	dictation; to dictate
6.	两	☐	huán	☐	inside
7.	还	☐	láidào	☐	interjection particle
8.	来到	☐	liǎng	☐	man
9.	时间	☐	lǐbian	☐	man
10.	里边	☐	nán	☐	on one's body
11.	男	☐	nánháir	☐	other
12.	男人	☐	nánpéngyou	☐	other people
13.	男生	☐	nánrén	☐	schoolboy
14.	男朋友	☐	nánshēng	☐	time
15.	男孩儿	☐	nǐmen	☐	to arrive
16.	听见	☐	shēnshang	☐	to find
17.	听写	☐	shēntǐ	☐	to go, to walk
18.	听到	☐	shíjiān	☐	to hear
19.	吧	☐	tīngdào	☐	to hear
20.	别人	☐	tīng//jiàn	☐	to look for
21.	别的	☐	tīngxiě	☐	to return; to pay back
22.	告诉	☐	zhǎo	☐	to tell
23.	你们	☐	zhǎodào	☐	to walk
24.	身上	☐	zǒu	☐	two, both
25.	身体	☐	zǒu//lù	☐	you (Pl.)

Once ready, check your solution with the help of the previous page.

Find the Chinese characters belonging to the following Pinyin words. In the grid, words with multiple characters can appear either vertically from top to bottom, or horizontally from left to right.

ba	huán	nánháir	shēnshang	tīngxiě
biéde	láidào	nánpéngyou	shēntǐ	zhǎo
biérén	liǎng	nánrén	shíjiān	zhǎodào
gàosu	lǐbian	nánshēng	tīngdào	zǒu
huài	nán	nǐmen	tīngjiàn	zǒulù

里	好	西	别	的	早	听	机	男	人	记	吧
边	看	汉	字	去	上	到	票	用	你	生	气
右	男	朋	友	年	身	火	走	白	们	包	后
边	半	生	电	认	体	车	路	介	绍	男	边
听	分	病	中	真	牛	奶	车	找	生	孩	北
写	本	还	学	听	见	从	票	到	日	儿	边
先	子	有	男	不	对	出	来	中	文	天	半
男	人	的	生	回	到	飞	时	间	打	球	年
过	西	边	元	书	身	地	在	家	也	别	人
两	包	子	走	店	上	上	坏	一	起	开	页
动	来	到	下	马	路	找	地	告	网	玩	问
作	喜	欢	次	找	风	到	图	诉	上	笑	男

A few Hanzi belonging to the Pinyin words above can be found twice in the grid. Take one of the pairs and insert them into the empty spaces below so that you get a meaningful sentence.

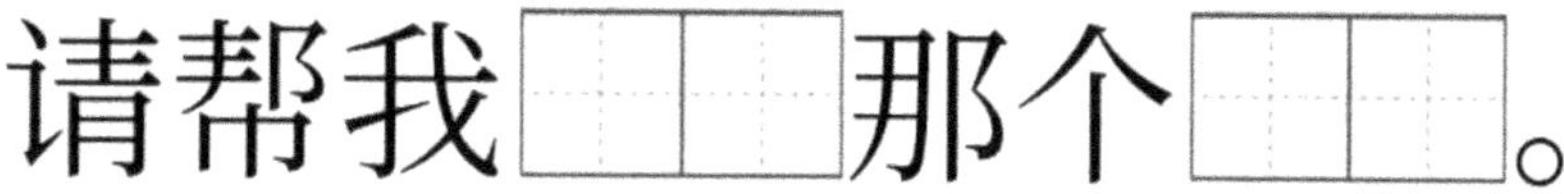

Put the English translation of the Chinese words into the squares. If the English translation contains more than one word, you must enter them without space into the squares.

Across

1 告诉   12 还
5 别人   13 身体
6 男孩儿   14 里边
7 找到   15 别的
10 听写   17 听见

Down

2 找
3 走   9 男人
4 男朋友   11 来到
6 坏   13 两
8 你们   16 时间

UNIT 15
Fill-in

Complete the crossword by entering the Pinyin of the supplied Chinese words.
This time, instead of providing you with clear indications as to where
the words should go, we show you hints of the tones in some of the squares.

坏 _______
找 _______
找到 _______
走 _______
走路 _______
两 _______
还 _______
来到 _______
吧 _______

时间 _______
里边 _______
男 _______
男人 _______
男生 _______
男朋友 _______
男孩儿 _______
听见 _______

听写 _______
听到 _______
别人 _______
别的 _______
告诉 _______
你们 _______
身上 _______
身体 _______

UNIT 15
QUIZ

Choose the correct answer.

1. *Bad* is

    a. huāi   b. huái   c. huài   d. huǎi

2. *To find* is

    a. zhǎodào   b. zhǎodǎo   c. zhàodǎo   d. zhàodáo

3. *Other people* is

    a. biērén   b.biérèn   c. biērèn   d.biérén

4. *Boyfriend* is

    a.nànpèngyou   b. nánpēngyou   c. nànpéngyou   d.nánpéngyou

5. *Two/both* is

    a.liàng   b. liǎng   c. liāng   d.liáng

6. *To arrive* is

    a. láidào   b. lāidào   c. làidào   d. làidāo

7. *Body* is

    a.shēntǐ   b. shèntǐ   c. shēntí   d. shènti

8. *Time* is

    a. shǐjián   b. shǐjiān   c. shíjián   d. shíjiān

9. *To walk* is

    a.zōulú   b. zǒulù   c. zōulú   d. zǒulū

10. *Dictation* is

    a. tíngxié   b. tīngxié   c. tīngxiě   d. tíngxiē

UNIT 16
VOCABULARY

1.	坐下	zuòxia	to sit down
2.	饭	fàn	rice; meal
3.	饭店	fàndiàn	restaurant
4.	床	chuáng	bed
5.	这儿	zhèr	here
6.	这边	zhèbiān	here
7.	这里	zhè•lǐ	here
8.	这些	zhèxiē	these
9.	忘	wàng	to forget
10.	忘记	wàngjì	to forget
11.	间	jiān	between; measure w. for rooms
12.	弟弟	dìdi	younger brother
13.	汽车	qìchē	car
14.	没什么	méi shénme	It's nothing.
15.	没有	méi•yǒu	to not have; no
16.	没事儿	méi//shìr	It's okay.
17.	快	kuài	fast
18.	鸡蛋	jīdàn	egg
19.	杯	bēi	cup
20.	到	dào	to reach
21.	非常	fēicháng	very
22.	国	guó	country; state; nation
23.	国外	guó wài	external; overseas; abroad
24.	国家	guójiā	country
25.	明年	míngnián	next year

UNIT 16
Matching exercise

Match the Hanzi with the corresponding Pinyin and English translation.

	Hanzi		Pinyin		English
1.	坐下	☐	bēi	☐	bed
2.	饭	☐	chuáng	☐	between; measure w. for rooms
3.	饭店	☐	dào	☐	car
4.	床	☐	dìdi	☐	country
5.	这儿	☐	fàn	☐	country; state; nation
6.	这边	☐	fàndiàn	☐	cup
7.	这里	☐	fēicháng	☐	egg
8.	这些	☐	guó	☐	external; overseas; abroad
9.	忘	☐	guójiā	☐	fast
10.	忘记	☐	guó wài	☐	here
11.	间	☐	jiān	☐	here
12.	弟弟	☐	jīdàn	☐	here
13.	汽车	☐	kuài	☐	It's nothing.
14.	没什么	☐	méi shénme	☐	It's okay.
15.	没有	☐	méi//shìr	☐	next year
16.	没事儿	☐	méi•yǒu	☐	restaurant
17.	快	☐	míngnián	☐	rice; meal
18.	鸡蛋	☐	qìchē	☐	these
19.	杯	☐	wàng	☐	to forget
20.	到	☐	wàngjì	☐	to forget
21.	非常	☐	zhèbiān	☐	to not have; no
22.	国	☐	zhè•lǐ	☐	to reach
23.	国外	☐	zhèr	☐	to sit down
24.	国家	☐	zhèxiē	☐	very
25.	明年	☐	zuòxia	☐	younger brother

Once ready, check your solution with the help of the previous page.

UNIT 16
Word search

Find the Chinese characters belonging to the following Pinyin words. In the grid, words with multiple characters can appear either vertically from top to bottom, or horizontally from left to right.

bēi	fàndiàn	jiān	méiyǒu	zhèbiān
chuáng	fēicháng	jīdàn	míngnián	zhèlǐ
dào	guó	kuài	qìchē	zhèr
dìdi	guójiā	méi shénme	wàng	zhèxiē
fàn	guó wài	méishìr	wàngjì	zuòxia

```
找 到 没 西 右 杯 关 上 没 早 记 住
床 问 有 边 这 早 忘 次 事 饭 坐 下
白 鸡 去 回 儿 上 记 有 儿 外 边 休
天 蛋 年 来 电 影 院 时 从 奶 这 息
忘 风 汽 车 马 饭 中 候 没 手 边 远
页 弟 门 口 路 店 文 车 什 机 下 间
手 弟 书 国 家 考 里 边 么 好 班 也
毛 认 包 老 告 试 弟 弟 比 玩 没 有
到 真 饭 人 诉 东 边 白 国 儿 号 中
不 大 动 马 汽 电 快 网 上 这 里 学
国 吃 这 上 车 视 地 非 常 行 正 明
外 饭 些 有 名 机 点 百 进 来 在 年
```

A few Hanzi belonging to the Pinyin words above can be found twice in the grid. Take one of the pairs and insert them into the empty spaces below so that you get a meaningful sentence.

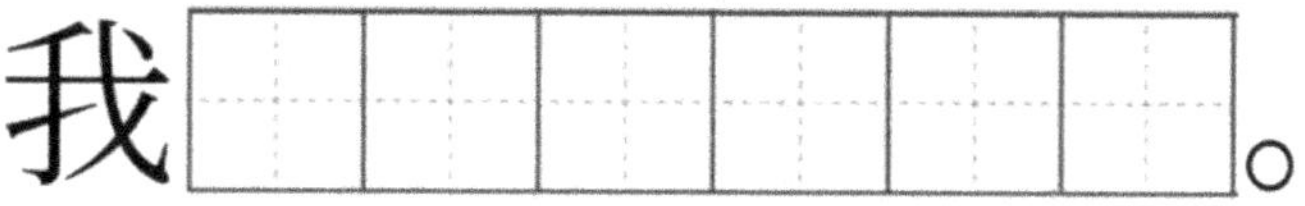

Put the English translation of the Chinese words into the squares. If the English translation contains more than one word, you must enter them without space into the squares.

Across

3 间

4 到

5 坐下

7 这些

9 忘

10 汽车

11 饭

12 快

13 国家

14 这里

16 国外

Down

1 明年

2 弟弟

3 床

4 饭店

6 没有

8 鸡蛋

10 杯

15 非常

Complete the crossword by entering the Pinyin of the supplied Chinese words.
This time, instead of providing you with clear indications as to where
the words should go, we show you hints of the tones in some of the squares.

坐下 _________

饭 _________

饭店 _________

床 _________

这儿 _________

这边 _________

这里 _________

这些 _________

忘 _________

忘记 _________

间 _________

弟弟 _________

汽车 _________

没什么 _________

没有 _________

没事儿 _________

快 _________

鸡蛋 _________

杯 _________

到 _________

非常 _________

国 _________

国外 _________

国家 _________

明年 _________

Choose the correct answer.

1. *Very* is

    a. fēicháng   b. fèichǎng   c. fēichǎng   d. fèichāng

2. *Country* is

    a. guǒjià   b. guōjiā   c. guójiā   d. guōjià

3. *Restaurant* is

    a. fàndiǎn   b. fǎndiàn   c.fāndiǎn   d.fàndiàn

4. *Egg* is

    a. jídān   b. jīdàn   c.jīdán   d. jīdān

5. *Next year* is

    a. mīngniàn   b. míngnián   c. mǐngnián   d. mǐngniàn

6. *To not have* is

    a. méiyóu   b. měiyóu   c. méiyǒu   d. měiyǒu

7. *To forget* is

    a. wāngjí   b. wǎngjí   c. wàngjì   d. wāngjì

8. *Here* is

    a. zhèlǐ   b. zhélǐ   c. zhélì   d. zhèlí

9. *These* is

    a. zhèxiě   b. zhěxiē   c. zhèxiē   d. zhěxié

10. *To sit down* is

    a. zuǒxiá   b. zuōxià   c. zuǒxià   d. zuòxia

REVISION
Characters

Create Chinese characters from the components.

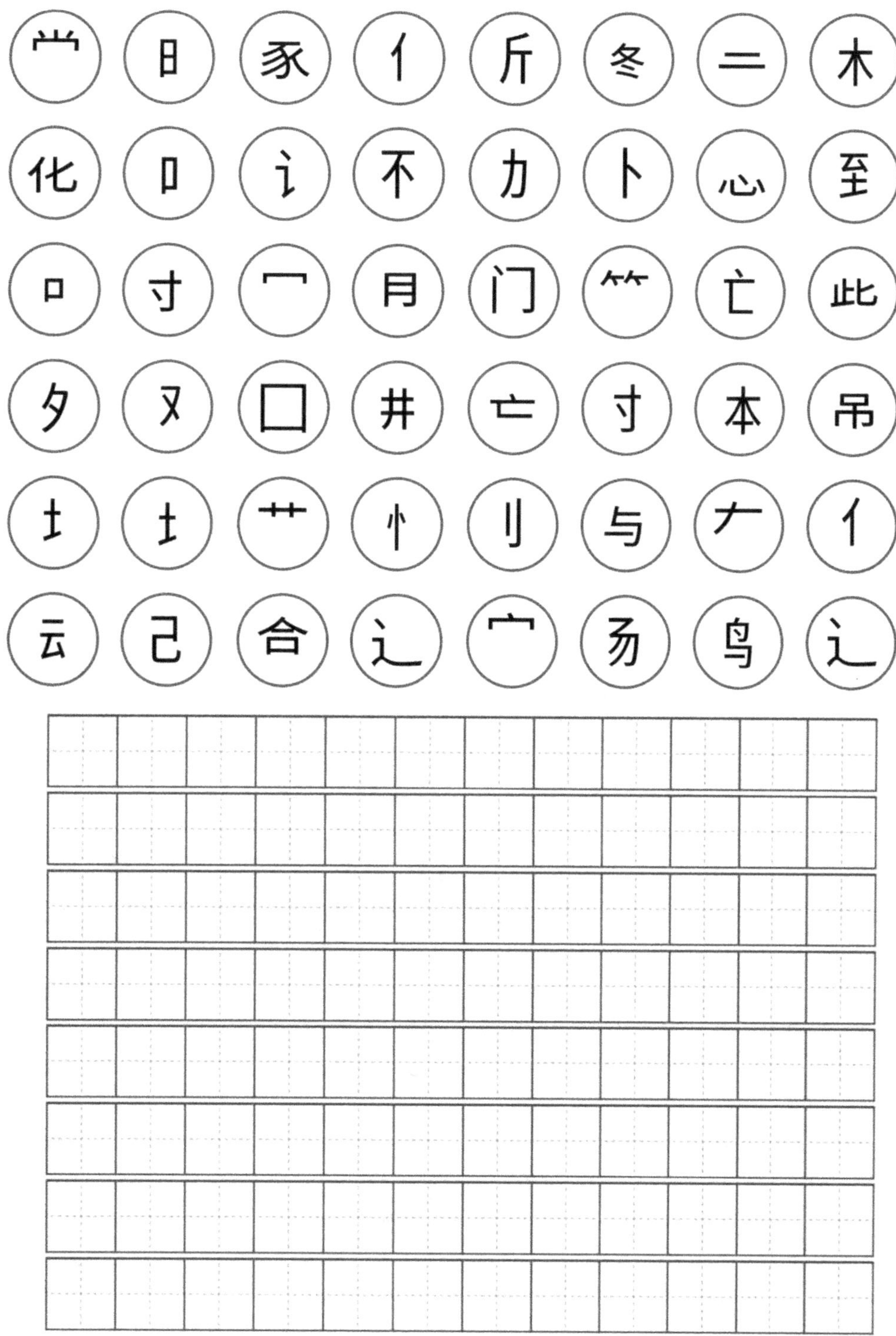

Match the Chinese words with the pictures.

考试　　肉　　饭店
老人　　休息　　床
地图　　问　　汽车
机场　　走路　　快
机票　　花　　鸡蛋
百　　男　　杯
吃饭　　男孩儿

REVISION
Crossword

Put the Pinyin into the squares.

Across

1 爷爷
4 这儿
6 百
9 早
10 还有
11 早上
13 远
14 回答
17 国
20 考试
22 间
23 还是
26 男朋友
28 回家
30 男
32 有用
34 出去
35 地
36 对
37 记
38 关
40 问
43 你们
46 别的
48 奶奶
49 告诉
50 动
52 进
54 走路
55 这些
56 休息
57 有些
58 这里

Down

2 有时
3 网友
4 在家
5 肉
7 床
8 考
9 找
12 身上
15 没有
16 行
17 国家
18 好玩儿
19 还
21 先
24 进去
25 花
27 过
29 机场
31 鸡蛋
32 有的
33 次
35 弟弟
39 男孩儿
40 忘记
41 奶
42 老
44 忙
45 回来
46 吧
47 地
50 到
51 页
53 那里
54 在
55 走

REVISION
Crossword

Put the Pinyin into the squares.

REVISION
Fill in

Complete the crossword by entering the Pinyin of the supplied Chinese words.
This time, instead of providing you with clear indications as to where
the words should go, we show you hints of the tones in some of the squares.

<table>
<tr><td>汉字</td><td>__________</td><td>坏</td><td>__________</td></tr>
<tr><td>记住</td><td>__________</td><td>两</td><td>__________</td></tr>
<tr><td>动作</td><td>__________</td><td>还</td><td>__________</td></tr>
<tr><td>老人</td><td>__________</td><td>时间</td><td>__________</td></tr>
<tr><td>地方</td><td>__________</td><td>里边</td><td>__________</td></tr>
<tr><td>地图</td><td>__________</td><td>男人</td><td>__________</td></tr>
<tr><td>地点</td><td>__________</td><td>男生</td><td>__________</td></tr>
<tr><td>机票</td><td>__________</td><td>听见</td><td>__________</td></tr>
<tr><td>西</td><td>__________</td><td>听写</td><td>__________</td></tr>
<tr><td>西边</td><td>__________</td><td>听到</td><td>__________</td></tr>
<tr><td>早饭</td><td>__________</td><td>别人</td><td>__________</td></tr>
<tr><td>吃饭</td><td>__________</td><td>身体</td><td>__________</td></tr>
<tr><td>回去</td><td>__________</td><td>坐下</td><td>__________</td></tr>
<tr><td>回到</td><td>__________</td><td>饭</td><td>__________</td></tr>
<tr><td>网上</td><td>__________</td><td>饭店</td><td>__________</td></tr>
<tr><td>后</td><td>__________</td><td>这边</td><td>__________</td></tr>
<tr><td>后天</td><td>__________</td><td>汽车</td><td>__________</td></tr>
<tr><td>后边</td><td>__________</td><td>没什么</td><td>__________</td></tr>
<tr><td>关上</td><td>__________</td><td>没事儿</td><td>__________</td></tr>
<tr><td>那儿</td><td>__________</td><td>快</td><td>__________</td></tr>
<tr><td>好吃</td><td>__________</td><td>杯</td><td>__________</td></tr>
<tr><td>好听</td><td>__________</td><td>非常</td><td>__________</td></tr>
<tr><td>好看</td><td>__________</td><td>国外</td><td>__________</td></tr>
<tr><td>进来</td><td>__________</td><td>明年</td><td>__________</td></tr>
</table>

REVISION
Fill in

Put the Pinyin into the squares.

REVISION
Group the Words

Group the words according to their meaning.

别人, 弟弟, 地方, 非常, 告诉, 好玩儿, 后边, 后天,
回来, 进去, 里边, 明年, 那边, 奶奶, 男朋友, 时间, 听见,
网友, 忘记, 西边, 爷爷, 有时候, 早, 找, 这边, 走

Verb	Location	People	Time	NONE

UNIT 17
VOCABULARY

1.	玩儿	wánr	to play
2.	事	shì	thing
3.	雨	yǔ	rain
4.	明白	míngbai	to understand; clear
5.	图书馆	túshūguǎn	library
6.	知识	zhīshi	knowledge
7.	知道	zhī•dào	to know
8.	放	fàng	to put down, to let go
9.	放学	fàng//xué	to be off school; classes are over
10.	放假	fàng//jià	to have a holiday
11.	学	xué	to learn; to study
12.	学院	xuéyuàn	college; academy
13.	试	shì	to try
14.	房子	fángzi	house; building
15.	房间	fángjiān	room
16.	话	huà	word; talk
17.	妹妹	mèimei	younger sister
18.	姐姐	jiějie	elder sister
19.	帮	bāng	to help, to assist
20.	帮忙	bāng máng	to help, to do a favour
21.	面包	miànbāo	bread
22.	面条儿	miàntiáor	noodles
23.	贵	guì	expensive
24.	看到	kàndào	to see; to notice
25.	看病	kàn//bìng	to see a doctor; to see a patient

Match the Hanzi with the corresponding Pinyin and English translation.

	Hanzi		Pinyin		English
1.	玩儿	☐	bāng	☐	bread
2.	事	☐	bāng máng	☐	college; academy
3.	雨	☐	fàng	☐	elder sister
4.	明白	☐	fàng//jià	☐	expensive
5.	图书馆	☐	fángjiān	☐	house; building
6.	知识	☐	fàng//xué	☐	knowledge
7.	知道	☐	fángzi	☐	library
8.	放	☐	guì	☐	noodles
9.	放学	☐	huà	☐	rain
10.	放假	☐	jiějie	☐	room
11.	学	☐	kàn//bìng	☐	thing
12.	学院	☐	kàndào	☐	to be off school; classes are over
13.	试	☐	mèimei	☐	to have a holiday
14.	房子	☐	miànbāo	☐	to help, to assist
15.	房间	☐	miàntiáor	☐	to help, to do a favour
16.	话	☐	míngbai	☐	to know
17.	妹妹	☐	shì	☐	to learn; to study
18.	姐姐	☐	shì	☐	to play
19.	帮	☐	túshūguǎn	☐	to put down, to let go
20.	帮忙	☐	wánr	☐	to see a doctor; to see a patient
21.	面包	☐	xué	☐	to see; to notice
22.	面条儿	☐	xuéyuàn	☐	to try
23.	贵	☐	yǔ	☐	to understand; clear
24.	看到	☐	zhī•dào	☐	word; talk
25.	看病	☐	zhīshi	☐	younger sister

Once ready, check your solution with the help of the previous page.

Find the Chinese characters belonging to the following Pinyin words. In the grid, words with multiple characters can appear either vertically from top to bottom, or horizontally from left to right.

bāng	fàngxué	kànbìng	míngbai	xué
bāng máng	fángzi	kàndào	shì	xuéyuàn
fàng	guì	mèimei	shì	yǔ
fàngjià	huà	miànbāo	túshūguǎn	zhīdào
fángjiān	jiějie	miàntiáor	wánr	zhīshi

早	上	姐	地	北	边	右	知	回	答	贵	肉
面	西	姐	方	房	认	边	识	老	学	身	图
条	出	来	考	子	真	正	在	人	院	上	书
儿	电	看	病	书	店	玩	中	见	比	手	馆
记	影	电	视	机	日	儿	文	妹	妹	地	百
得	院	进	看	中	期	牛	奶	下	班	图	放
生	放	去	到	间	告	北	学	早	知	那	些
日	学	本	子	也	诉	火	车	饭	道	网	友
雨	回	去	房	间	马	明	号	话	用	姐	姐
山	放	假	见	面	上	白	手	机	出	对	过
事	东	边	打	球	帮	上	网	面	包	再	远
毛	图	书	馆	从	忙	门	试	风	东	半	帮

A few Hanzi belonging to the Pinyin words above can be found twice in the grid. Take one of the pairs and insert them into the empty spaces below so that you get a meaningful sentence.

他的　□□　想要在　□□□　工作。

Put the English translation of the Chinese words into the squares. If the English translation contains more than one word, you must enter them without space into the squares.

Across

1 姐姐
4 玩儿
5 看到
6 面包
8 放学
12 话
14 帮忙
15 明白
16 面条儿
17 试
19 妹妹
21 帮
22 知识

Down

2 放
3 放假
7 房间
9 学院
10 图书馆
11 看病
12 事
13 学
18 房子
20 雨

UNIT 17
Fill-in

Complete the crossword by entering the Pinyin of the supplied Chinese words.
This time, instead of providing you with clear indications as to where
the words should go, we show you hints of the tones in some of the squares.

玩儿 ______

事 ______

雨 ______

明白 ______

图书馆 ______

知识 ______

知道 ______

放学 ______

放假 ______

学 ______

学院 ______

房子 ______

房间 ______

话 ______

妹妹 ______

姐姐 ______

帮 ______

帮忙 ______

面包 ______

面条儿 ______

贵 ______

看到 ______

看病 ______

Choose the correct answer.

1. *To help* is
a. bāng māng   b. bǎng máng   c. báng mǎng   d. bāng máng

2. *To have a holiday* is
a. fǎngjià   b. fàngjià   c.fángjiǎ   d.fāngjiá

3. *Room* is
a. fāngjiān   b. fángjiǎn   c. fángjiān   d.fǎngjiàn

4. *Expensive* is
a. guī   b. guì   c. guǐ   d. guí

5. *Elder sister* is
a. jiějie   b. jiējie   c. jiéjie   d. jièjie

6. *To see a doctor* is
a. kánbǐng   b. kànbǐng   c. kánbìng   d. kànbìng

7. *Noodles* is
a. miàntiàor   b. miántiàor   c. miàntiáor   d. miāntiáor

8. *Thing* is
a. shǐ   b. shí   c. shī   d. shì

9. *Rain* is
a. yǔ   b. yú   c. yū   d.yù

10. *To know* is
a. zhídǎo   b. zhǐdǎo   c. zhǐdǎo   d. zhīdào

UNIT 18
VOCABULARY

1.	南	nán	south
2.	南边	nánbian	south; the southern side
3.	树	shù	tree
4.	要	yào	to want
5.	是不是	shì bu shì	is or isn't; isn't it?
6.	星期天	xīngqītiān	Sunday
7.	星期日	xīngqīrì	Sunday
8.	哪儿	nǎr	where
9.	哪里	nǎ•lǐ	where
10.	哪些	nǎxiē	which ones
11.	重	zhòng	heavy
12.	差	chà	difference; short of
13.	送	sòng	to deliver; to give as a present
14.	前	qián	front; ago
15.	前天	qiántiān	the day before yesterday
16.	前边	qiánbian	in front
17.	洗	xǐ	to wash
18.	觉得	juéde	to feel; to think
19.	穿	chuān	to wear
20.	说	shuō	to speak
21.	孩子	háizi	children
22.	给	gěi	to give
23.	班	bān	class
24.	起	qǐ	to get up; to start; to rise
25.	起来	qǐ//•lái	to stand up

UNIT 18
Matching exercise

Match the Hanzi with the corresponding Pinyin and English translation.

	Hanzi		Pinyin		English
1.	南	☐	bān	☐	children
2.	南边	☐	chà	☐	class
3.	树	☐	chuān	☐	difference; short of
4.	要	☐	gěi	☐	front; ago
5.	是不是	☐	háizi	☐	heavy
6.	星期天	☐	juéde	☐	in front
7.	星期日	☐	nǎ•lǐ	☐	is or isn't; isn't it?
8.	哪儿	☐	nǎxiē	☐	south
9.	哪里	☐	nán	☐	south; the southern side
10.	哪些	☐	nánbian	☐	Sunday
11.	重	☐	nǎr	☐	Sunday
12.	差	☐	qǐ	☐	the day before yesterday
13.	送	☐	qián	☐	to deliver; to give as a present
14.	前	☐	qiánbian	☐	to feel; to think
15.	前天	☐	qiántiān	☐	to get up; to start; to rise
16.	前边	☐	qǐ//•lái	☐	to give
17.	洗	☐	shì bu shì	☐	to speak
18.	觉得	☐	shù	☐	to stand up
19.	穿	☐	shuō	☐	to want
20.	说	☐	sòng	☐	to wash
21.	孩子	☐	xǐ	☐	to wear
22.	给	☐	xīngqīrì	☐	tree
23.	班	☐	xīngqītiān	☐	where
24.	起	☐	yào	☐	where
25.	起来	☐	zhòng	☐	which ones

Once ready, check your solution with the help of the previous page.

Find the Chinese characters belonging to the following Pinyin words. In the grid, words with multiple characters can appear either vertically from top to bottom, or horizontally from left to right.

bān	juéde	nǎr	qǐlái	xǐ
chà	nǎlǐ	qǐ	shì bu shì	xīngqīrì
chuān	nǎxiē	qián	shù	xīngqītiān
gěi	nán	qiánbian	shuō	yào
háizi	nánbian	qiántiān	sòng	zhòng

树 朋 有 时 候 网 孩 子 再 男 哪 生
没 友 星 期 天 上 好 包 送 人 里 气
有 们 地 早 考 要 听 差 外 穿 半 天
前 边 上 说 试 记 别 好 玩 儿 南 边
吃 东 重 生 起 住 是 不 是 弟 回 去
饭 班 车 日 打 开 肉 手 机 弟 给 生
南 热 票 哪 儿 开 洗 听 写 起 身 病
找 星 牛 马 上 玩 干 机 上 来 体 地
到 期 奶 菜 起 笑 什 票 课 中 前 图
想 天 一 孩 喜 欢 么 哪 些 学 下 次
开 会 会 子 读 漂 亮 学 校 生 工 前
觉 得 儿 谁 请 星 期 日 现 在 人 天

A few Hanzi belonging to the Pinyin words above can be found twice in the grid. Take one of the pairs and insert them into the empty spaces below so that you get a meaningful sentence.

你的 ☐☐☐☐☐ 什么时候☐床?

Put the English translation of the Chinese words into the squares. If the English translation contains more than one word, you must enter them without space into the squares.

Across

2 差
4 给
5 要
7 南
8 觉得
9 送
10 洗
11 前边
13 哪里
15 起来
16 班

Down

1 起
3 孩子
5 哪些
6 树
7 说
12 重
13 穿
14 星期天

140

Complete the crossword by entering the Pinyin of the supplied Chinese words.
This time, instead of providing you with clear indications as to where
the words should go, we show you hints of the tones in some of the squares.

南　＿＿＿＿＿　　　　　　　　　　洗　＿＿＿＿＿

南边　＿＿＿＿＿　　　哪里　＿＿＿＿＿　　觉得　＿＿＿＿＿

树　＿＿＿＿＿　　　　哪些　＿＿＿＿＿　　穿　＿＿＿＿＿

要　＿＿＿＿＿　　　　重　＿＿＿＿＿　　　说　＿＿＿＿＿

是不是　＿＿＿＿＿　　差　＿＿＿＿＿　　　孩子　＿＿＿＿＿

星期天　＿＿＿＿＿　　送　＿＿＿＿＿　　　给　＿＿＿＿＿

星期日　＿＿＿＿＿　　前天　＿＿＿＿＿　　班　＿＿＿＿＿

哪儿　＿＿＿＿＿　　　前边　＿＿＿＿＿　　起来　＿＿＿＿＿

UNIT 18
QUIZ

Choose the correct answer.

1. *To wear* is

    a. chuán   b. chuǎn   c. chuān   d. chuàn

2. *To give* is

    a. gēi   b. gěi   c. géi   d. gèi

3. *Which ones* is

    a. náxiè   b. nǎxiè   c. nàxiē   d. nǎxiē

4. *The day before yesterday* is

    a. qiàntiǎn   b. qiántiān   c. qiǎntiàn   d. qiǎntiān

5. *To stand up* is

    a. qǐlái   b. qǐlǎi   c. qìlái   d. qìlāi

6. *To speak* is

    a. shuǒ   b. shuō   c. shuò   d. shuó

7. *Tree* is

    a. shū   b. shú   c. shǔ   d. shù

8. *To deliver/to give as a present* is

    a. sòng   b. sōng   c. sóng   d. sǒng

9. *To want* is

    a. yào   b. yǎo   c. yāo   d. yáo

10. *To wash* is

    a. xì   b. xī   c. xǐ   d. xí

UNIT 19
VOCABULARY

1.	重要	zhòngyào	important
2.	洗手间	xǐshǒujiān	restroom
3.	起床	qǐ//chuáng	to get up
4.	真	zhēn	real, true
5.	真的	zhēn de	really
6.	哥哥	gēge	elder brother
7.	钱包	qiánbāo	wallet
8.	笑	xiào	to laugh
9.	拿	ná	to take
10.	爱好	àihào	hobby
11.	饿	è	hungry
12.	高	gāo	high, tall
13.	准备	zhǔnbèi	to get ready
14.	病	bìng	disease
15.	病人	bìngrén	sick person, patient
16.	站	zhàn	to stand; station
17.	旁边	pángbiān	side
18.	家人	jiārén	family member
19.	家里	jiā li	at home
20.	读书	dú//shū	to read; to study
21.	课	kè	course; lesson
22.	教	jiāo	to teach
23.	教学楼	jiàoxuélóu	classroom building
24.	常	cháng	ordinary; often
25.	常常	chángcháng	frequently; often

Match the Hanzi with the corresponding Pinyin and English translation.

	Hanzi		Pinyin		English
1.	重要	☐	àihào	☐	at home
2.	洗手间	☐	bìng	☐	classroom building
3.	起床	☐	bìngrén	☐	course; lesson
4.	真	☐	cháng	☐	disease
5.	真的	☐	chángcháng	☐	elder brother
6.	哥哥	☐	dú//shū	☐	family member
7.	钱包	☐	è	☐	frequently; often
8.	笑	☐	gāo	☐	high, tall
9.	拿	☐	gēge	☐	hobby
10.	爱好	☐	jiā li	☐	hungry
11.	饿	☐	jiāo	☐	important
12.	高	☐	jiàoxuélóu	☐	ordinary; often
13.	准备	☐	jiārén	☐	real, true
14.	病	☐	kè	☐	really
15.	病人	☐	ná	☐	restroom
16.	站	☐	pángbiān	☐	sick person, patient
17.	旁边	☐	qiánbāo	☐	side
18.	家人	☐	qǐ//chuáng	☐	to get ready
19.	家里	☐	xiào	☐	to get up
20.	读书	☐	xǐshǒujiān	☐	to laugh
21.	课	☐	zhàn	☐	to read; to study
22.	教	☐	zhēn	☐	to stand; station
23.	教学楼	☐	zhēn de	☐	to take
24.	常	☐	zhòngyào	☐	to teach
25.	常常	☐	zhǔnbèi	☐	wallet

Once ready, check your solution with the help of the previous page

UNIT 19
Word search

Find the Chinese characters belonging to the following Pinyin words. In the grid, words with multiple characters can appear either vertically from top to bottom, or horizontally from left to right.

àihào	dúshū	jiāo	pángbiān	zhàn
bìng	è	jiàoxuélóu	qiánbāo	zhēn
bìngrén	gāo	jiārén	qǐchuáng	zhēn de
cháng	gēge	kè	xiào	zhòngyào
chángcháng	jiā li	ná	xǐshǒujiān	zhǔnbèi

常	记	门	口	笑	谁	开	爸	爸	真	的	时
山	得	见	面	喂	拿	会	站	坐	椅	字	候
北	重	想	哥	哥	下	病	喜	准	子	家	里
边	要	电	影	院	边	人	欢	备	怎	饭	馆
教	一	起	洗	手	间	医	生	生	么	课	电
同	钱	包	苹	果	左	读	书	日	样	和	视
学	来	不	用	起	钱	书	店	洗	手	间	机
电	爱	没	好	床	朋	对	不	起	正	在	医
话	好	关	今	年	友	常	常	车	旁	边	院
真	火	系	家	人	中	介	绍	上	星	马	哥
分	车	高	她	明	学	教	学	楼	期	上	哥
做	睡	觉	饿	天	生	开	玩	笑	病	不	对

A few Hanzi belonging to the Pinyin words above can be found twice in the grid. Take one of the pairs and insert them into the empty spaces below so that you get a meaningful sentence.

我 ☐☐ 很快就要去 ☐☐☐ 了。

Put the English translation of the Chinese words into the squares. If the English translation contains more than one word, you must enter them without space into the squares.

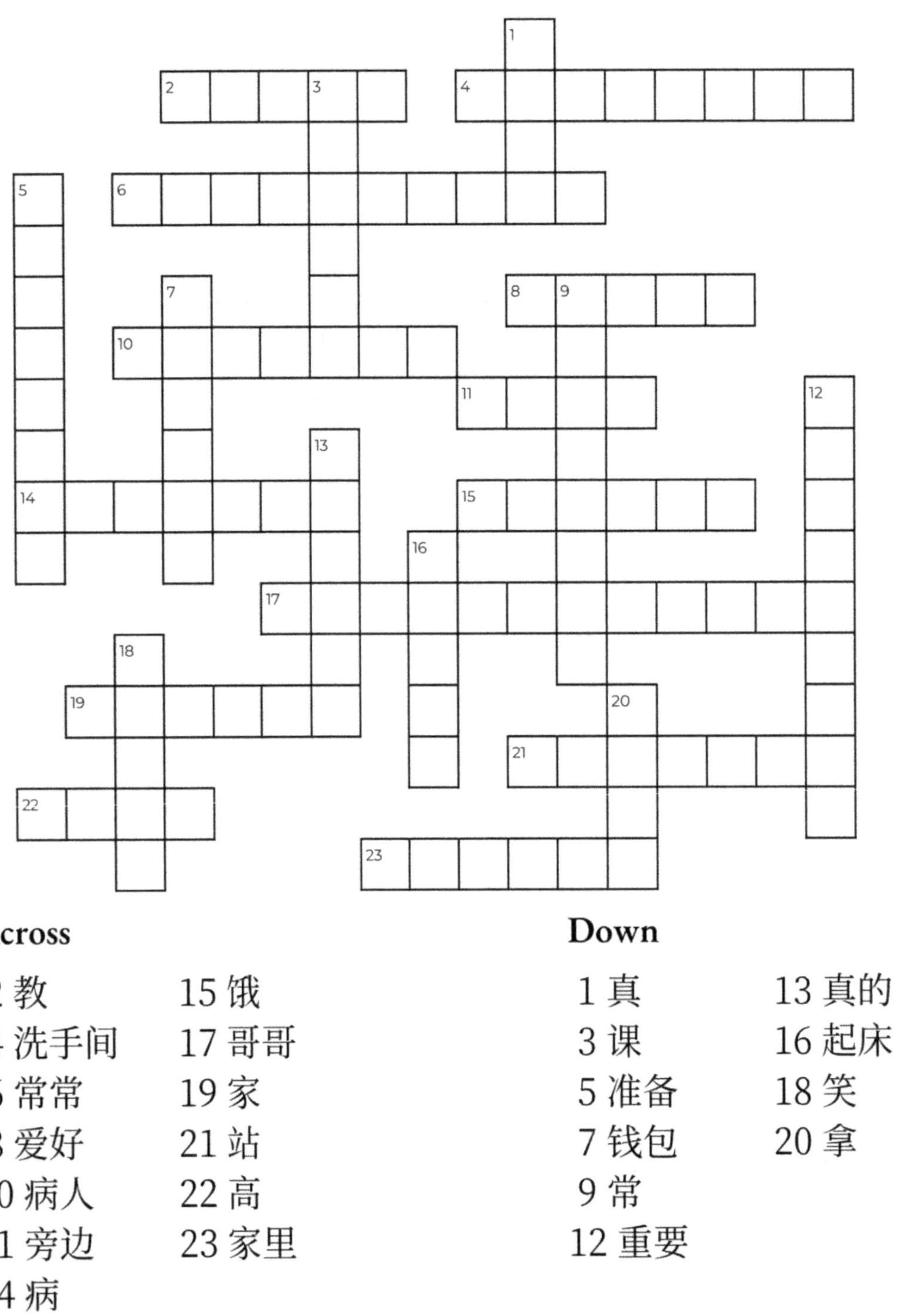

Across

2 教
4 洗手间
6 常常
8 爱好
10 病人
11 旁边
14 病
15 饿
17 哥哥
19 家
21 站
22 高
23 家里

Down

1 真
3 课
5 准备
7 钱包
9 常
12 重要
13 真的
16 起床
18 笑
20 拿

UNIT 19
Fill-in

Complete the crossword by entering the Pinyin of the supplied Chinese words.
This time, instead of providing you with clear indications as to where
the words should go, we show you hints of the tones in some of the squares.

重要 _____	笑 _____	旁边 _____
洗手间 _____	拿 _____	家人 _____
起床 _____	爱好 _____	读书 _____
真 _____	高 _____	教 _____
真的 _____	准备 _____	教学楼 _____
哥哥 _____	病人 _____	常 _____
钱包 _____	站 _____	常常 _____

UNIT 19
QUIZ

Choose the correct answer.

1. *Hobby* is

    a. àihào   b. āiháo   c. àiháo   d. àihǎo

2. *To read/to study* is

    a. dùshū   b. dúshù   c. dúshū   d. dǔshǔ

3. *High/tall* is

    a. gǎo   b. gāo   c. gào   d. gáo

4. *To take* is

    a. ná   b. nā   c. nǎ   d. nà

5. *At home* is

    a. jiǎ lì   b. jiā li   c. jiá lì   d. jià lí

6. *To teach* is

    a. jiào   b. jiǎo   c. jiáo   d. jiāo

7. *Wallet* is

    a. qiǎnbǎo   b. qiānbào   c. qiánbāo   d. qiànbáo

8. *To get up* is

    a. qǐchuàng   b. qǐchuáng   c. qìchuáng   d. qìchuāng

9. *To laugh* is

    a. xiāo   b. xiào   c. xiáo   d. xiǎo

10. *To get ready* is

    a. zhúnbēi   b. zhūnbéi   c. zhùnběi   d. zhǔnbèi

1.	请问	qǐngwèn	excuse me
2.	请进	qǐng jìn	please come in
3.	请坐	qǐng zuò	please have a seat
4.	请假	qǐng//jià	to ask for leave
5.	课文	kèwén	text
6.	课本	kèběn	textbook
7.	难	nán	hard, difficult
8.	球	qiú	ball
9.	票	piào	ticket
10.	晚	wǎn	late
11.	晚上	wǎnshang	(in the) evening, (at) night
12.	晚饭	wǎnfàn	dinner
13.	累	lèi	tired
14.	唱	chàng	to sing
15.	唱歌	chàng//gē	to sing a song
16.	第二	dì èr	second
17.	您	nín	you (courteous)
18.	得到	dé//dào	to get, to obtain
19.	商场	shāngchǎng	mall; shopping mall
20.	商店	shāngdiàn	shop
21.	着	zhe	in process of
22.	最	zuì	intensifier of adjectives, most
23.	最后	zuìhòu	last
24.	最好	zuìhǎo	best
25.	跑	pǎo	to run

UNIT 20
Matching exercise

Match the Hanzi with the corresponding Pinyin and English translation.

	Hanzi		Pinyin		English
1.	请问	☐	chàng	☐	ball
2.	请进	☐	chàng//gē	☐	best
3.	请坐	☐	dé//dào	☐	dinner
4.	请假	☐	dì èr	☐	excuse me
5.	课文	☐	kèběn	☐	hard, difficult
6.	课本	☐	kèwén	☐	in process of
7.	难	☐	lèi	☐	(in the) evening, (at) night
8.	球	☐	nán	☐	intensifier of adjectives, most
9.	票	☐	nín	☐	last
10.	晚	☐	pǎo	☐	late
11.	晚上	☐	piào	☐	mall; shopping mall
12.	晚饭	☐	qǐng//jià	☐	please come in
13.	累	☐	qǐng jìn	☐	please have a seat
14.	唱	☐	qǐngwèn	☐	second
15.	唱歌	☐	qǐng zuò	☐	shop
16.	第二	☐	qiú	☐	text
17.	您	☐	shāngchǎng	☐	textbook
18.	得到	☐	shāngdiàn	☐	ticket
19.	商场	☐	wǎn	☐	tired
20.	商店	☐	wǎnfàn	☐	to ask for leave
21.	着	☐	wǎnshang	☐	to get, to obtain
22.	最	☐	zhe	☐	to run
23.	最后	☐	zuì	☐	to sing
24.	最好	☐	zuìhǎo	☐	to sing a song
25.	跑	☐	zuìhòu	☐	you (courteous)

UNIT 20
Word search

Find the Chinese characters belonging to the following Pinyin words. In the grid, words with multiple characters can appear either vertically from top to bottom, or horizontally from left to right.

chàng	kèwén	piào	qiú	wǎnshang
chànggē	lèi	qǐngjià	shāngchǎng	zhe
dédào	nán	qǐng jìn	shāngdiàn	zuì
dì èr	nín	qǐngwèn	wǎn	zuìhǎo
kèběn	pǎo	qǐng zuò	wǎnfàn	zuìhòu

星	请	坐	时	课	南	边	房	子	非	常	试
期	回	去	间	本	这	儿	雨	第	二	重	贵
天	商	店	好	还	还	您	汽	车	觉	两	球
票	里	边	玩	有	晚	来	课	文	得	明	白
包	累	坐	儿	唱	早	到	找	饭	事	快	放
最	听	下	帮	歌	上	最	后	店	得	到	学
好	见	商	忙	班	着	先	好	最	关	身	放
房	间	场	哪	好	吃	那	看	好	起	体	假
请	问	面	些	国	晚	些	难	没	再	请	假
知	道	包	请	外	饭	回	家	事	网	友	国
学	跑	前	进	休	息	唱	回	儿	西	最	家
院	给	天	花	商	店	话	答	晚	上	听	到

A few Hanzi belonging to the Pinyin words above can be found twice in the grid. Take one of the pairs and insert them into the empty spaces below so that you get a meaningful sentence.

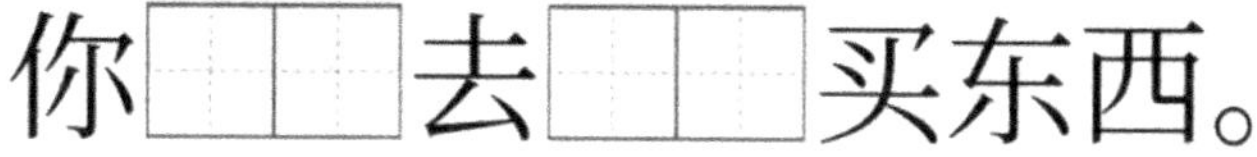

151

Put the English translation of the Chinese words into the squares. If the English translation contains more than one word, you must enter them without space into the squares.

Across

2 您

4 第二   11 最

7 难   14 最好

8 球   16 累

9 唱歌   19 晚上

10 晚   20 票

Down

1 请假

3 得到   13 课文

5 请问   15 商店

6 商场   17 跑

7 晚饭   18 最后

12 课本

Complete the crossword by entering the Pinyin of the supplied Chinese words.
This time, instead of providing you with clear indications as to where
the words should go, we show you hints of the tones in some of the squares.

请问 _________   票 _________   您 _________

请进 _________   晚 _________   得到 _________

请坐 _________   晚上 _________   商场 _________

请假 _________   晚饭 _________   商店 _________

课文 _________   累 _________   着 _________

课本 _________   唱 _________   最 _________

难 _________   唱歌 _________   最后 _________

球 _________   第二 _________   最好 _________

                                          跑 _________

UNIT 20
QUIZ

Choose the correct answer.

1. *To get/to obtain* is

    a. dédào   b. dèdào   c. dēdáo   d. dédāo

2. *Text* is

    a. kēwén   b. kēwén   c. kèwén   d. kěwèn

3. *Tired* is

    a. lèi   b. lěi   c. lēi   d. léi

4. *Hard/difficult* is

    a. nān   b. nán   c. nàn   d. năn

5. *To run* is

    a. pào   b. păo   c. pāo   d. páo

6. *Please come in* is

    a. qīng jín   b. qǐng jín   c. qìng jīn   d. qǐng jìn

7. *Shopping mall* is

    a. shángchăng   b. shāngchăng   c. shăngchāng   d. shángcháng

8. *Shop* is

    a. shángdiàn   b. shăngdiān   c. shāngdián   d. shāngdiàn

9. *Dinner* is

    a. wānfăn   b. wánfăn   c. wānfàn   d. wănfàn

10. *Best* is

    a. zuíhāo   b. zuíhào   c. zuìhǎo   d. zuìhào

UNIT 21
VOCABULARY

1.	等	děng	to wait
2.	就	jiù	as soon as; right away; then
3.	渴	kě	thirsty
4.	楼	lóu	floor
5.	楼下	lóu xià	downstairs
6.	楼上	lóu shàng	upstairs
7.	睡	shuì	to sleep
8.	路	lù	road
9.	路上	lùshang	on the road
10.	路口	lùkǒu	intersection; crossing
11.	跟	gēn	with
12.	错	cuò	wrong, mistaken
13.	新	xīn	new
14.	新年	xīnnián	New Year
15.	歌	gē	song
16.	慢	màn	slow

Match the Hanzi with the corresponding Pinyin and English translation.

1.	等	cuò		as soon as; right away; then
2.	就	děng		downstairs
3.	渴	gē		floor
4.	楼	gēn		intersection; crossing
5.	楼下	jiù		new
6.	楼上	kě		New Year
7.	睡	lóu		on the road
8.	路	lóu shàng		road
9.	路上	lóu xià		slow
10.	路口	lù		song
11.	跟	lùkǒu		thirsty
12.	错	lùshang		to sleep
13.	新	màn		to wait
14.	新年	shuì		upstairs
15.	歌	xīn		with
16.	慢	xīnnián		wrong, mistaken

Once ready, check your solution with the help of the previous page.

UNIT 21
Word search

Find the Chinese characters belonging to the following Pinyin words. In the grid, words with multiple characters can appear either vertically from top to bottom, or horizontally from left to right.

cuò	gēn	lóu	lùkǒu	shuì
děng	jiù	lóu shàng	lùshang	xīn
gē	kě	lóu xià	màn	xīnnián
		lù		

<table>
<tr><td>拿</td><td>慢</td><td>钱</td><td>包</td><td>新</td><td>家</td><td>里</td><td>走</td><td>房</td><td>读</td><td>新</td><td>高</td></tr>
<tr><td>请</td><td>病</td><td>给</td><td>南</td><td>知</td><td>是</td><td>不</td><td>是</td><td>子</td><td>书</td><td>年</td><td>找</td></tr>
<tr><td>问</td><td>人</td><td>楼</td><td>上</td><td>道</td><td>洗</td><td>等</td><td>饿</td><td>路</td><td>走</td><td>路</td><td>到</td></tr>
<tr><td>错</td><td>机</td><td>这</td><td>听</td><td>写</td><td>手</td><td>回</td><td>肉</td><td>进</td><td>楼</td><td>下</td><td>后</td></tr>
<tr><td>差</td><td>场</td><td>里</td><td>路</td><td>口</td><td>间</td><td>到</td><td>常</td><td>去</td><td>星</td><td>期</td><td>日</td></tr>
<tr><td>身</td><td>再</td><td>外</td><td>国</td><td>早</td><td>就</td><td>男</td><td>常</td><td>页</td><td>考</td><td>渴</td><td>有</td></tr>
<tr><td>体</td><td>电</td><td>楼</td><td>地</td><td>上</td><td>火</td><td>朋</td><td>跟</td><td>风</td><td>试</td><td>动</td><td>名</td></tr>
<tr><td>路</td><td>影</td><td>生</td><td>方</td><td>北</td><td>车</td><td>友</td><td>教</td><td>打</td><td>球</td><td>歌</td><td>先</td></tr>
<tr><td>口</td><td>院</td><td>气</td><td>起</td><td>等</td><td>左</td><td>看</td><td>学</td><td>生</td><td>放</td><td>家</td><td>人</td></tr>
<tr><td>觉</td><td>西</td><td>睡</td><td>床</td><td>半</td><td>晚</td><td>病</td><td>楼</td><td>病</td><td>路</td><td>远</td><td>记</td></tr>
<tr><td>得</td><td>边</td><td>有</td><td>爷</td><td>天</td><td>下</td><td>后</td><td>行</td><td>贵</td><td>上</td><td>好</td><td>得</td></tr>
<tr><td>跟</td><td>百</td><td>用</td><td>网</td><td>上</td><td>次</td><td>边</td><td>关</td><td>上</td><td>还</td><td>吃</td><td>花</td></tr>
</table>

A few Hanzi belonging to the Pinyin words above can be found twice in the grid. Take one of the pairs and insert them into the empty spaces below so that you get a meaningful sentence.

我☐孩子们下楼来了，我们在☐☐☐着你。

UNIT 21
Crossword

Put the English translation of the Chinese words into the squares. If the English translation contains more than one word, you must enter them without space into the squares.

Across

2 错
6 渴
8 慢
9 歌
11 等
12 路
13 楼上

Down

1 路口
3 新年
4 楼下
5 跟
6 就
7 睡
10 楼

UNIT 21
Fill-in

Complete the crossword by entering the Pinyin of the supplied Chinese words.
This time, instead of providing you with clear indications as to where
the words should go, we show you hints of the tones in some of the squares.

等 ______	路上 ______
就 ______	路口 ______
渴 ______	跟 ______
楼 ______	错 ______
楼下 ______	新 ______
楼上 ______	新年 ______
睡 ______	慢 ______

UNIT 21
QUIZ

Choose the correct answer.

1. *Wrong* is

    a. cuō   b. cuǒ   c. cuò   d. cuó

2. *To wait* is

    a. déng   b. děng   c. dēng   d. dèng

3. *Song* is

    a. gē   b. gè   c. gé   d. gě

4. *With* is

    a. gěn   b. gēn   c. gén   d.gèn

5. *Thirsty* is

    a. kè   b. kě   c. kē   d. ké

6. *Upstairs* is

    a. lōu shàng   b. lǒu shàng   c. lòu shàng   d. lóu shàng

7. *Crossing* is

    a. lūkǒu   b. lùkǒu   c. lúkòu   d. lǔkǒu

8. *Slow* is

    a. màn   b. mān   c. mǎn   d. mán

9. *To sleep* is

    a. shuǐ   b. shuì   c. shuí   d. shuī

10. *New* is

    a. xín   b. xǐn   c. xīn   d. xìn

REVISION
Characters

Create Chinese characters from the components.

氵 忄 垂 包 隹 丷 广 又
免 彳 寺 饣 刂 对 见 口
先 钅 方 纟 曼 覀 只 完
⺌ 日 昔 讠 户 辶 月 阝
合 木 宀 曷 足 木 首 矢
我 牙 寻 ⺮ 氵 示 兑 讠

Match the Chinese words with the pictures.

☐ 雨 ☐ 钱包 ☐ 商店
☐ 房子 ☐ 笑 ☐ 跑
☐ 房间 ☐ 病人 ☐ 楼下
☐ 树 ☐ 读书 ☐ 楼上
☐ 面包 ☐ 课本 ☐ 睡
☐ 面条儿 ☐ 晚上 ☐ 慢
☐ 孩子们 ☐ 唱歌

REVISION
Crossword puzzle

Write the Pinyin into the squares.

Across

2 病人
5 就
6 累
7 起床
10 给
11 看到
14 洗
15 帮
16 最后
17 路口
18 钱
20 雨
21 路上
22 新
23 南
24 起
25 票
26 准备
27 孩子
28 楼上
30 明白
33 错
34 晚

35 球
36 要
38 着
39 知道
41 真
44 新年
45 跑

Down

1 放
3 跟
4 哪儿
5 家
6 楼
7 前边
8 话
9 高
12 哪里
13 唱
14 学院
16 最好
19 南边
22 学
24 钱包
28 楼下
29 事
30 慢
31 哥哥
32 读书
34 玩儿
37 爱好
38 站

40 第
42 您
43 难

Write the Pinyin into the squares.

REVISION
Fill in

Complete the crossword by entering the Pinyin of the supplied Chinese words.
This time, instead of providing you with clear indications as to where
the words should go, we show you hints of the tones in some of the squares.

图书馆	_____________	真的	_____________
知识	_____________	笑	_____________
放学	_____________	旁边	_____________
放假	_____________	家人	_____________
房子	_____________	请问	_____________
房间	_____________	请进	_____________
妹妹	_____________	请坐	_____________
姐姐	_____________	请假	_____________
帮忙	_____________	课	_____________
树	_____________	课文	_____________
面包	_____________	课本	_____________
面条儿	_____________	教	_____________
是不是	_____________	教学楼	_____________
星期天	_____________	常	_____________
星期日	_____________	常常	_____________
贵	_____________	晚饭	_____________
哪些	_____________	唱歌	_____________
看病	_____________	得到	_____________
重要	_____________	商场	_____________
送	_____________	最	_____________
洗手间	_____________	等	_____________
觉得	_____________	渴	_____________
穿	_____________	睡	_____________
说	_____________	歌	_____________
起来	_____________		

Write the Pinyin into the squares.

Group the words according to their meaning.

明白, 图书馆, 知识, 学院, 试, 妹妹, 姐姐, 星期日, 贵, 重要,
前天, 前边, 洗, 洗手间, 给, 起床, 哥哥, 拿, 高, 病人, 旁边,
难, 教学楼, 累, 商场, 最, 渴, 路口, 新

Verb	Location	People	Adjective	NONE

SOLUTIONS

UNIT 1

Character search

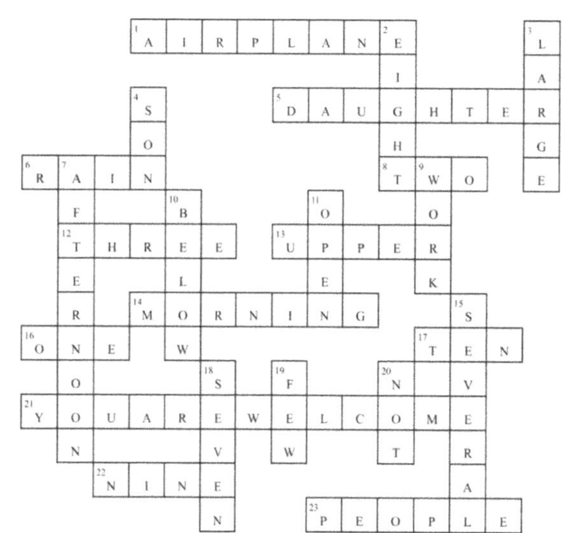

今天下午下了很大的雨。

Crossword

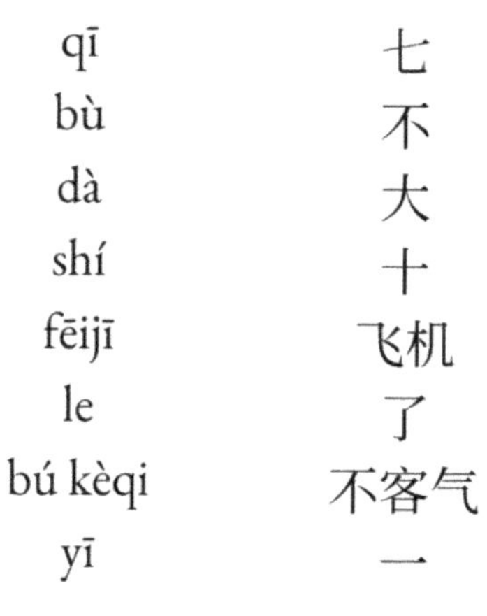

Word Fill in

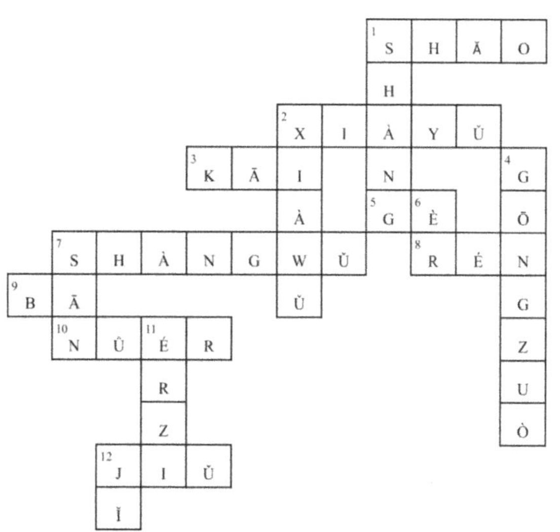

Letter Cloud

qī   七
bù   不
dà   大
shí   十
fēijī   飞机
le   了
bú kèqi   不客气
yī   一

bā 八 eight

UNIT 2

Character search

我今天中午在火车站前面等你。

Crossword

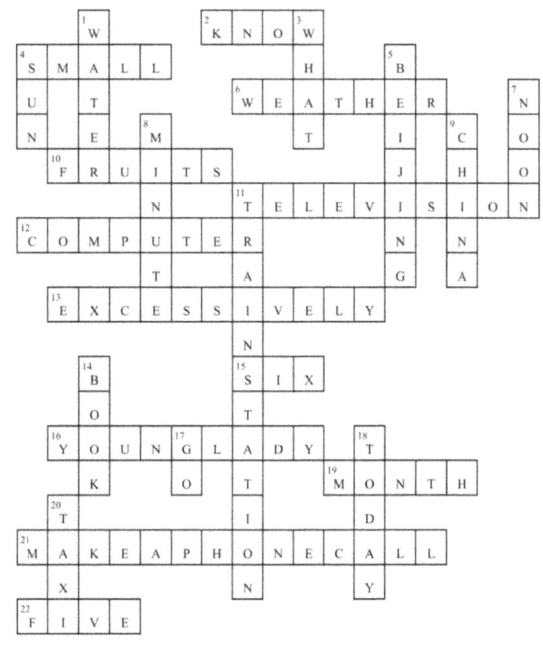

Word Fill in

Letter Cloud

qù

shū

yuè

liù

shuǐ

xiǎo

wǔ

rì

去 书 月 六 水 小 五 日

tài 太 too, excessively

UNIT 3

Character search

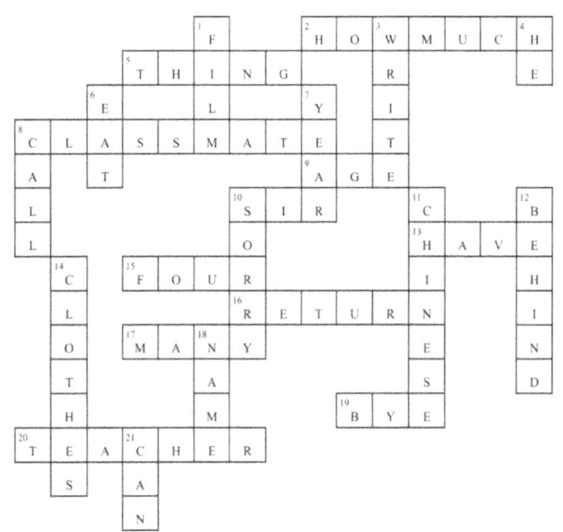

你叫什么名字?

Crossword

Word Fill in

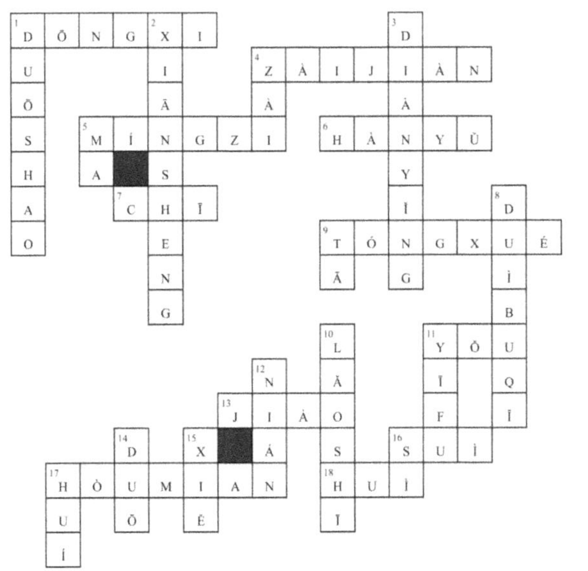

Letter Cloud

yǒu	有
yīfu	衣服
míngzi	名字
nián	年
jiào	叫
chī	吃
duō	多
xiě	写

huí 回 to return

UNIT 4

Character search

我的妈妈明天去医院。

Crossword

Word Fill in

Letter Cloud

lái	来
mǎi	买
tīng	听
wǒ	我
yīshēng	医生
lěng	冷
nǐ	你
píngguǒ	苹果

hǎo 好 good

UNIT 5

Character search

<table>
<tr><td>名</td><td>字</td><td>昨</td><td>回</td><td>同</td><td>高</td><td>中</td><td>叫</td><td>汉</td><td>些</td><td>会</td><td>吗</td></tr>
<tr><td>这</td><td>吃</td><td>天</td><td>去</td><td>学</td><td>兴</td><td>国</td><td>茶</td><td>语</td><td>飞</td><td>她</td><td>点</td></tr>
<tr><td>先</td><td>中</td><td>午</td><td>开</td><td>的</td><td>电</td><td>脑</td><td>今</td><td>爸</td><td>机</td><td>小</td><td>姐</td></tr>
<tr><td>生</td><td>学</td><td>生</td><td>不</td><td>对</td><td>不</td><td>起</td><td>天</td><td>爸</td><td>五</td><td>很</td><td>七</td></tr>
<tr><td>朋</td><td>卜</td><td>雨</td><td>狗</td><td>不</td><td>星</td><td>期</td><td>四</td><td>打</td><td>个</td><td>衣</td><td>服</td></tr>
<tr><td>友</td><td>爱</td><td>上</td><td>午</td><td>客</td><td>再</td><td>见</td><td>很</td><td>电</td><td>朋</td><td>十</td><td>火</td></tr>
<tr><td>认</td><td>小</td><td>太</td><td>是</td><td>气</td><td>大</td><td>住</td><td>水</td><td>话</td><td>友</td><td>六</td><td>车</td></tr>
<tr><td>识</td><td>和</td><td>水</td><td>果</td><td>高</td><td>兴</td><td>九</td><td>的</td><td>本</td><td>天</td><td>气</td><td>站</td></tr>
<tr><td>狗</td><td>分</td><td>钟</td><td>学</td><td>女</td><td>儿</td><td>现</td><td>写</td><td>哪</td><td>北</td><td>看</td><td>电</td></tr>
<tr><td>儿</td><td>少</td><td>上</td><td>习</td><td>什</td><td>块</td><td>在</td><td>月</td><td>后</td><td>京</td><td>东</td><td>视</td></tr>
<tr><td>子</td><td>学</td><td>那</td><td>妈</td><td>么</td><td>老</td><td>米</td><td>读</td><td>面</td><td>坐</td><td>西</td><td>好</td></tr>
<tr><td>日</td><td>校</td><td>来</td><td>年</td><td>都</td><td>师</td><td>饭</td><td>听</td><td>有</td><td>书</td><td>现</td><td>在</td></tr>
</table>

现在我朋友的狗很高兴。

Crossword

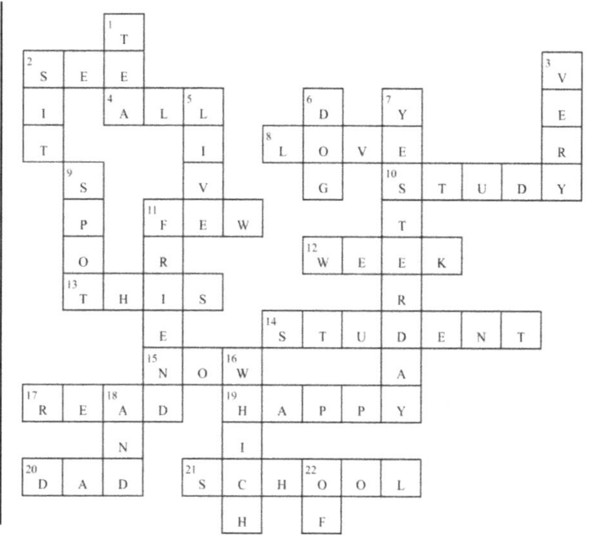

Word Fill in

to see	k	à	n

a few	x	i	ē

spot	d	i	ǎ	n

dad*	b	à	b	a

to be	s	h	i

to sit	z	u	ò

to love	à	i

happy	g	ā	o	x	i	n	g

all	d	ō	u

of*	d	e

tea	c	h	á

student	x	u	é	s	h	ē	n	g

very	h	ě	n

yesterday	z	u	ó	t	i	ā	n

to dwell*	z	h	ù

friend*	p	é	n	g	y	o	u

dog	g	ǒ	u

which	n	ǎ

to read	d	ú

to study	x	u	é	x	i

and	h	é

week	x	ī	n	g	q	ī

school*	x	u	é	x	i	à	o

now	x	i	à	n	z	à	i

Letter Cloud

zhè	这
zuò	坐
chá	茶
kàn	看
ài	爱
xuéxiào	学校
zuótiān	昨天
xiē	些

zhù　住　to live, to dwell

我爸爸的朋友住在学校旁边。

UNIT 6

Character search

我在商店前面看见了一只漂亮的猫。

Crossword

Word Fill in

Letter Cloud

qián	钱
qǐng	请
rè	热
shuōhuà	说话
zěnme	怎么
yǐzi	椅子
líng	零
shéi	谁

zuò 做 to do

REVISION

Creating Characters

狗, 你, 冷, 没, 很, 做, 钱, 块,
喂, 热, 能, 妈, 请, 都, 的

Matching

5	电视	11	钱	9	出租车
8	苹果	6	吃	16	朋友们
1	飞机	15	衣服	21	狗
13	书	3	打电话	2	下雨
18	桌子	12	买	10	妈妈
4	电脑	17	医生	20	猫
19	喝	7	电影	14	医院

Crossword

Word Fill-in

Group the Words

Number

八 九 零 六 七 十 四 五

Location

北京
饭馆
火车站
商店
学校
医院
中国

People

儿子
老师
女儿
朋友
同学
先生
学生
医生

Object

杯子
电脑
电视
书
衣服
椅子
桌子

None

吃
好
喝
很
冷
上午
昨天

UNIT 7

Character search

这些大学生一起上学。

Crossword

Word Fill in

Letter Cloud

gānjìng   干净
yíbàn   一半
shàng cì   上次
xià chē   下车
xiàbān   下班
yìqǐ   一起
dàxué   大学
gōngrén   工人

gàn   干   to do

UNIT 8

Character search

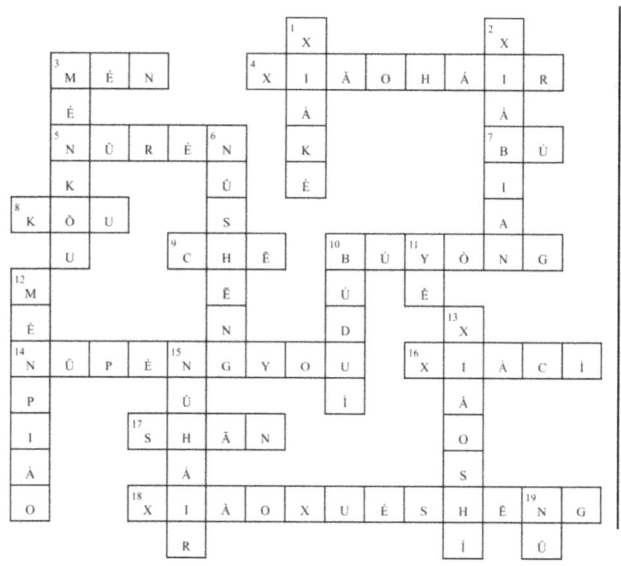

这些女人和那些小孩儿要
在小学的门口见面。

Crossword

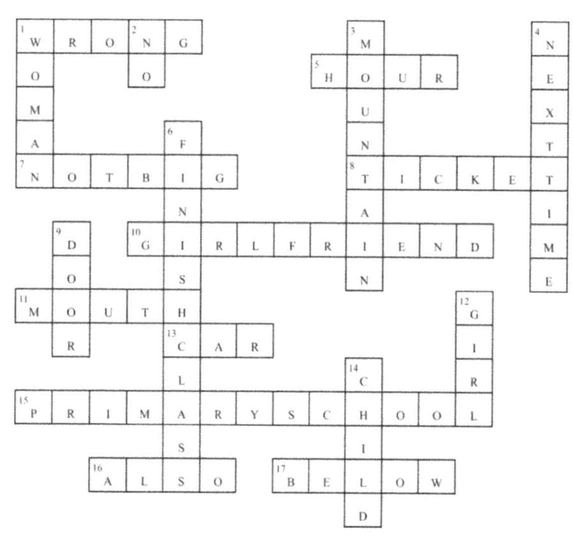

Word Fill in

Letter Cloud

yě	也
chē	车
xiǎoshí	小时
shān	山
kǒu	口
ménpiào	门票
nǚ	女
búduì	不对

xià cì　下次　next time

UNIT 9

Character search

这些老师和中学生马上要去火车站。

Crossword

Word Fill in

Letter Cloud

Zhōngwén	中文
rìqī	日期
tiān	天
shǒujī	手机
chēpiào	车票
fēi	飞
kāi//huì	开会
jiàn//miàn	见面

mǎlù　马路　road; street

UNIT 10

Character search

我的弟弟正在打车, 他要去电影院。

Crossword

Word Fill in

Letter Cloud

rènzhēn　认真
dōng　东
cóng　从
fēn　分
dǎ　打
jièshào　介绍
huǒ chē　火车
fēng　风

diàn　电　electricity

181

UNIT 11

Character search

去年我在国外生病了。

Crossword

Word Fill in

Quiz

1. To get angry a. shēngqì
2. Outside c. wàibian
3. To use c. yòng
4. Last year d. qùnián
5. Birthday b. shēngrì
6. Daytime a. báitiān
7. Right d. yòu
8. Number/date b. hào
9. Foreign country d. wàiguó
10. Foreign language c. wàiyǔ

REVISION

Creating Characters

打，对，站，别，球，话，视，影，
边，净，绍，玩，路，奶，孩，认，
次，课，病，饭，间，机，院，笑

Matching

12	工人	5	马路	2	书包
7	口	10	开会	20	书店
18	山	19	车	14	打球
15	门口	21	车站	4	本子
3	女	6	手	13	电视机
17	女孩儿	16	手机	1	包
11	飞	8	牛奶	9	包子

Crossword

Word Fill in

Group the Words

Time	Location	People
一会儿	一块儿	工人
小时	中间	大学生
马上	左	小孩儿
日期	右边	女朋友
今年	北边	中学生
去年	**Object**	**None**
半天	车票	风
	手机	打球
	本子	生气
	电视机	生病
	包	外语
		出来

UNIT 12

Character search

考试的地点在哪里?

Crossword

Word Fill in

Quiz

1. Movement b. dòngzuò
2. To go out d. chūqù
3. Grandma a. nǎinai
4. Place/location c. dìdiǎn
5. Air ticket b. jīpiào
6. Examination a. kǎoshì
7. Map d. dìtú
8. Airport b. jīchǎng
9. West side c. xībian
10. To pass time c. guò

UNIT 13

Character search

明天早上我不要在家吃饭。

Crossword

Word Fill in

Quiz

1. Again c. zài
2. To have meal b. chīfàn
3. To go back to d. huídào
4. Hundred c. bǎi
5. Page a. yè
6. Some/somewhat c. yǒuxiē
7. At home b. zàijiā
8. Useful c. yǒuyòng
9. Breakfast a. zǎofàn
10. Famous d. yǒumíng

UNIT 14

Character search

午饭后我爷爷要休息。

Crossword

Word Fill in

Quiz

1. Delicious d. hǎochī
2. Far b. yuǎn
3. To come in c. jìnlái
4. Busy b. máng
5. To rest a. xiūxi
6. To close/to shut a. guānshang
7. They d. tāmen
8. Flower c. huā
9. To ask a. wèn
10. There c. nàr

UNIT 15

Character search

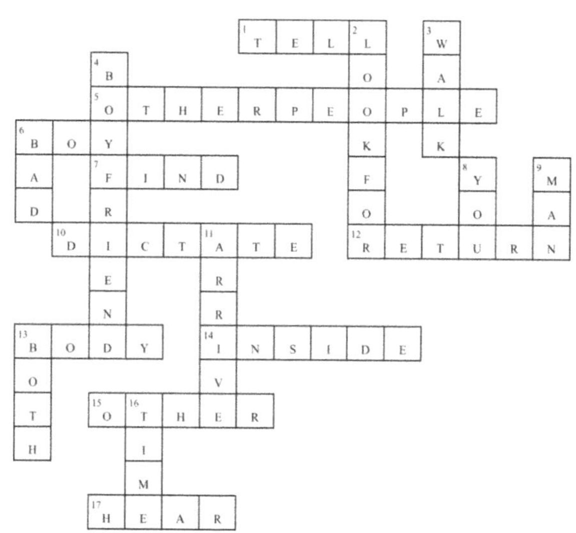

请帮我找到那个男人。

Crossword

Word Fill in

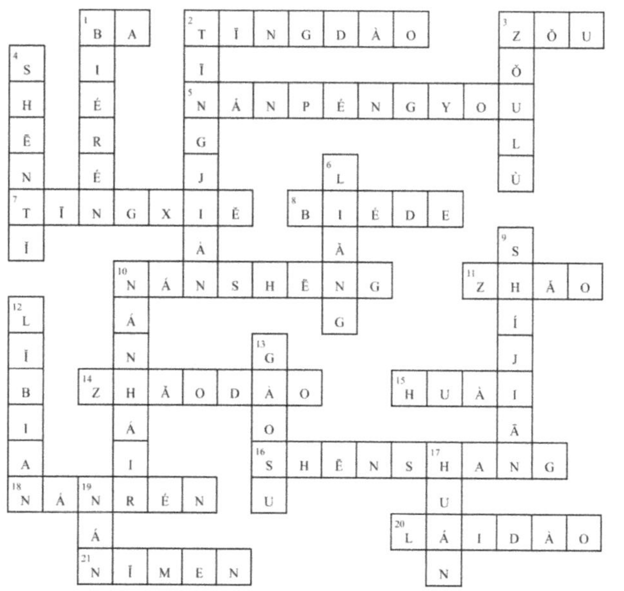

Quiz

1. Bad c. huài
2. To find a. zhǎodào
3. Other people d. biérén
4. Boyfriend d. nánpéngyou
5. Two/both b. liǎng
6. To arrive a. láidào
7. Body a. shēntǐ
8. Time d. shíjiān
9. To walk b. zǒulù
10. Dictation c. tīngxiě

UNIT 16

Character search

找	到	没	西	右	杯	关	上	没	早	记	住
床	间	有	边	这	早	忘	次	事	饭	坐	下
白	鸡	去	回	儿	上	记	有	儿	外	边	休
天	蛋	年	来	电	影	院	时	从	奶	这	息
忘	风	汽	车	马	饭	中	候	没	手	边	远
页	弟	门	口	路	店	文	车	什	机	下	间
手	弟	书	国	家	考	试	里	么	好	班	也
毛	认	包	老	告	试	弟	弟	比	玩	没	有
到	真	饭	人	诉	东	边	白	国	儿	号	中
不	大	动	马	汽	电	快	网	上	这	里	学
国	吃	这	上	车	视	地	非	常	行	正	明
外	饭	些	有	名	机	点	百	进	来	在	年

我弟弟没有汽车。

Crossword

Across:
3. BETWEEN
4. REACH
5. SIT DOWN
7. THESE
9. FORGET
10. CAR
11. RICE
12. FAST
13. COUNTRY
14. HERE
16. OVERSEAS

Word Fill in

Quiz

1. Very a. fēicháng
2. Country c. guójiā
3. Restaurant d. fàndiàn
4. Egg b. jīdàn
5. Next year b. míngnián
6. To not have c. méiyǒu
7. To forget c. wàngjì
8. Here a. zhèlǐ
9. These c. zhèxiē
10. To sit down d. zuòxia

REVISION

Creating Characters

动, 到, 过, 外, 家, 图, 有, 听,
常, 坏, 花, 答, 记, 场, 鸡, 进,
忙, 休, 些, 时, 体, 写, 忘, 问

Matching

13	考试	17	肉	18	饭店
15	老人	19	休息	11	床
16	地图	12	问	14	汽车
2	机场	20	走路	5	快
7	机票	1	花	10	鸡蛋
3	百	9	男	6	杯
8	吃饭	4	男孩儿		

Crossword

Word Fill in

Group the Words

Verb	Location	People
告诉	地方	别人
回来	后边	弟弟
进去	里边	奶奶
听见	那边	男朋友
忘记	西边	网友
找	这边	爷爷
走		

Time	None
后天	非常
明年	好玩儿
时间	
有时候	
早	

UNIT 17

Character search

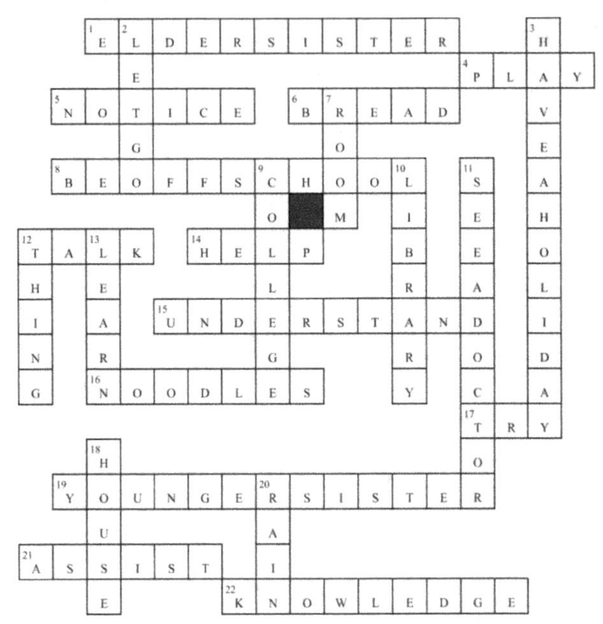

他的姐姐想要在图书馆工作。

Crossword

Word Fill in

Quiz

1. To help d. bāng máng
2. To have a holiday b. fàngjià
3. Room c. fángjiān
4. Expensive b. guì
5. Elder sister a. jiějie
6. To see a doctor d. kànbìng
7. Noodles c. miàntiáor
8. Thing d. shì
9. Rain a. yǔ
10. To know d. zhīdào

UNIT 18

Character search

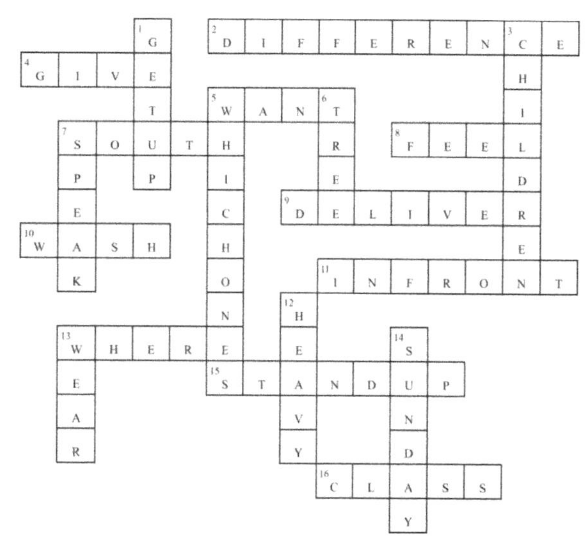

你的孩子星期天什么时候起床?

Crossword

Word Fill in

Quiz

1. To wear c. chuān
2. To give b. gěi
3. Which ones d. nǎxiē
4. The day before yesterday b. qiántiān
5. To stand up a. qǐlái
6. To speak b. shuō
7. Tree d. shù
8. To deliver/to give as a present a. sòng
9. To want a. yào
10. To wash c. xǐ

UNIT 19

Character search

我哥哥很快就要去教学楼了。

Crossword

Word Fill in

Quiz

1. Hobby a. àihào
2. To read/to study c. dúshū
3. High/tall b. gāo
4. To take a. ná
5. At home b. jiā li
6. To teach d. jiāo
7. Wallet c. qiánbāo
8. To get up b. qǐchuáng
9. To laugh b. xiào
10. To get ready d. zhǔnbèi

UNIT 20

Character search

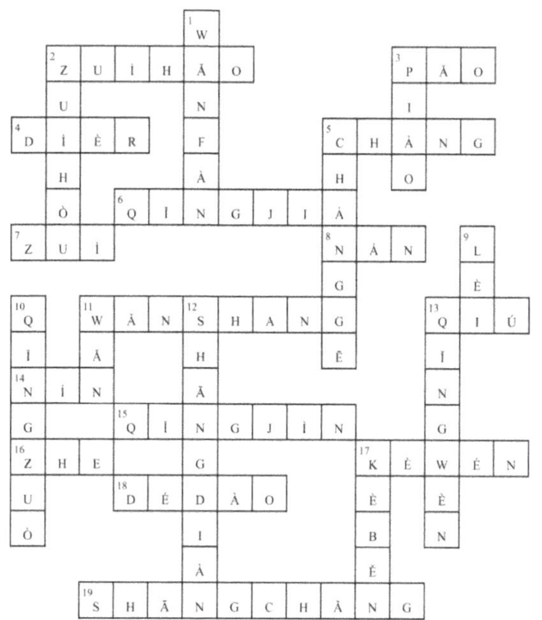

你最好去商店买东西。

Crossword

Word Fill in

Quiz

1. To get/to obtain a. dédào
2. Text c. kèwén
3. Tired a. lèi
4. Hard/difficult b. nán
5. To run b. pǎo
6. Please come in d. qǐng jìn
7. Shopping mall b. shāngchǎng
8. Shop d. shāngdiàn
9. Dinner d. wǎnfàn
10. Best c. zuìhǎo

193

UNIT 21

Character search

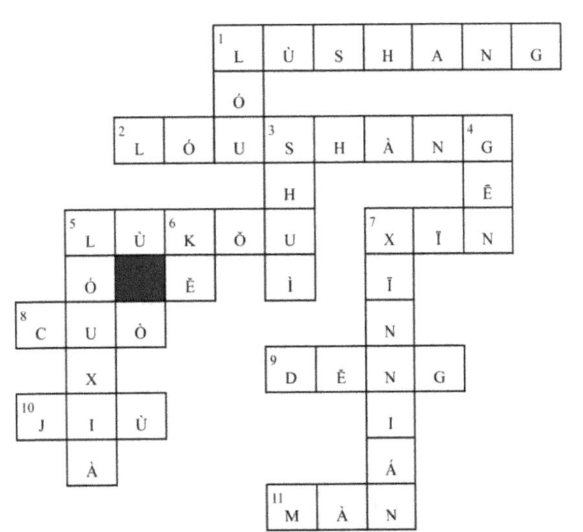

我跟孩子们下楼来了，
我们在路口等着你。

Crossword

Word Fill in

Quiz

1. Wrong c. cuò
2. To wait b. děng
3. Song a. gē
4. With b. gēn
5. Thirsty b. kě
6. Upstairs d. lóu shàng
7. Crossing b. lùkǒu
8. Slow a. màn
9. To sleep b. shuì
10. New c. xīn

194

REVISION

Creating Characters

穿，错，等，饿，房，给，觉，得，
渴，慢，难，跑，票，前，床，树，
睡，说，晚，洗，院，道，识，知

Matching

7	雨	15	钱包	12	商店
5	房子	13	笑	19	跑
20	房间	1	病人	3	楼下
16	树	4	读书	9	楼上
17	面包	2	课本	11	睡
10	面条儿	14	晚上	8	慢
18	孩子们	6	唱歌		

Crossword

Word Fill in

Group the Words

Verb
明白
试
洗
给
起床
拿

Adj.
贵
重要
高
难
累
渴
新

Location
图书馆
学院
前边
洗手间
旁边
教学楼
商场
路口

People
妹妹
姐姐
哥哥
病人

None
知识
星期日
前天
最

Wishing you success in your exams.

Elle Lin